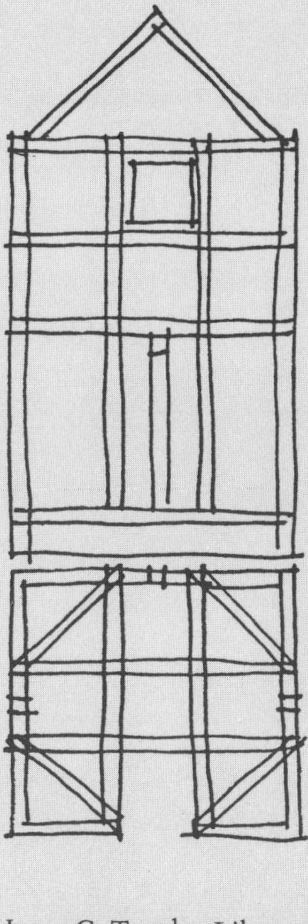

Bibliotheca Persica

Columbia Lectures
on Iranian Studies
Number 4

Religious Trends in Early Islamic Iran

Bibliotheca Persica consists of:

Persian Heritage Series, devoted to translations of Persian classics
Persian Studies Series, monographs on Iranian studies
Modern Persian Literature Series, devoted to translations of modern Persian writings
Columbia Lectures on Iranian Studies
Ṭabarī Translation, an annotated translation of al-Ṭabarī's *History*
Persian Texts Series, critical editions of Persian texts

Columbia Lectures on Iranian Studies

This series is intended to serve as a vehicle for the presentation of original research or synthesis in Iranian history and culture by distinguished scholars.

Volumes Already Published in the Series

Richard Ettinghausen and Ehsan Yarshater, eds., *Highlights of Persian Art,* 1979 (Bibliotheca Persica)

Sir Harold W. Bailey, *The Culture of the Sakas in Ancient Iranian Khotan,* 1982 (Bibliotheca Persica)

Ann K. S. Lambton, *Continuity and Change in Medieval Persia: Aspects of Administrative, Economic, and Social History, 11th–14th Century,* 1988 (SUNY Press)

Ehsan Yarshater, ed., *Persian Literature,* 1988 (SUNY Press)

Columbia Lectures on Iranian Studies

Edited by Ehsan Yarshater

Number 4

Religious Trends in Early Islamic Iran

Wilferd Madelung

The University of Oxford

Bibliotheca Persica

Published by

The Persian Heritage Foundation under
the imprint of Bibliotheca Persica

Printed in the United States of America

**For information, address State University of New York
Press, State University Plaza, Albany, N.Y., 12246**

Library of Congress Cataloging-in-Publication Data

Madelung, Wilferd.
Religious trends in early Islamic Iran.
(Columbia lectures on Iranian studies; no. 4)
(Bibliotheca Persica)
Bibliography: p.
Includes index.
1. Islam—Iran—History. 2. Islam—Iraq—History.
I. Title. II. Series. III. Series: Bibliotheca
Persica (Albany, N.Y.)
BP63.I67M33 1988 297′.0955 87–20975ISBN 0–88706–700–X
ISBN 0–88706–701–8 (pbk.)

10 9 8 7 6 5 4 3 2 1

Contents

Foreword

The present volume, the fourth in the series, is a study of aspects of religious trends and major sects in Iran in the early Islamic period, up to the Mongol invasion in the thirteenth century. Although the chapters are succinct, they represent a distillation of extensive research on the part of Professor Madelung, Laudian Professor of Arabic at the University of Oxford, and a foremost expert on the history of Islam in general and Shiʿite Islam and the Muʿtazilites in particular. In its comprehensiveness and authority, the volume can be considered a manual on Islamic sects in Iran before the fall of the Abbasid Caliphate.

Professor Madelung studied at the Universities of Georgetown, Cairo, Göttingen, and Hamburg. He received his Ph.D. degree in Arabic and Islamic history from the last institution. Before he was invited in 1979 to occupy his present chair at Oxford, he taught at the Universities of Texas, Hamburg, and Chicago.

Professor Madelung has written extensively on many aspects of Islamic thought and history, especially on Twelver, Zaidi, and Ismaili Shiʿism. His *Der Imam al-Qāsim ibn Ibrāhīm und die Glaubenslehre der Zaiditen* was published in Berlin in 1965. He is a distinguished contributor to various learned journals, and his authoritative articles have been published also in the *Encyclopaedia of Islam, Encyclopaedia Iranica,* and *Cambridge History of Iran.* A volume of his collected articles under the title *Religious Schools and Sects in Medieval Islam* was published in London in 1985. His *Arabic Texts on the History of Zaidī Imāms of Ṭabaristān, Daylamān and Gīlān* was published in Beirut in 1987.

Ehsan Yarshater
General Editor

Preface

The Arab conquest of Iran in the middle of the seventh century set off the most radical religious revolution in the country's history. The indigenous religious tradition which had developed a characteristic dualist worldview was broken and gradually supplanted by Islam, the latest of the monotheistic Semitic religions. Iran lost its national religious identity and became permanently merged into the much wider Islamic world. Its religious history since then has been merely an aspect of the general history of Islam. It has regularly reflected, and in turn influenced, developments elsewhere in the Islamic world.

The present chapters deal mainly with various currents and developments of Islam in Iran from its introduction to the Mongol conquest in the thirteenth century. These currents had to be cut to some extent from their wider Islamic context. The connections between the developments in Iran and in Mesopotamia, however, were often too close to be ignored. Mesopotamia had been part of the Persian empire before the rise of Islam and even contained the administrative capital of the Sassanian state. Although its native population was of Semitic stock and for the most part maintained its separate and varied religious traditions, it was also a natural environment for the rise of syncretistic movements amalgamating Iranian and local religious heritages which then radiated into Iran proper.

In early Islamic times the strong bonds between Mesopotamia and Iran persisted. Iran was conquered and garrisoned by Arabs who had first settled in Kufa and Basra and later maintained close ties with these two early centers of Islam in Iraq. Under the ʿAbbasids, who were brought to power by a religious movement which originated in Kufa and drew its military strength mainly from northeastern Iran, Baghdad in Iraq became the capital of Islam. Although it strove to control the world of Islam in all directions, its primary orientation was traditionally toward the east. It is not surprising then that most of the currents and developments discussed here, wherever they originated, sooner or later affected both Iran and Iraq. There were, however, also some exceptions to this rule and differences between the two regions which deserve to be noted.

The chapters contain the text, with only minor changes, of five Columbia Lectures on Iranian Studies presented in December 1983. Chapters 4 and 5, on Sufism and the Karrāmiyya and on Khārijism, have been added to these. The annotation has been generally kept to a minimum and, wherever possible, general studies have been referred to where references to the sources and full discussions of the issues may be found. Only in the chapter on Khārijism, where few relevant studies were available, a fuller annotation and discussion of the source reports seemed indispensable. It could not be the aim of this book to offer a survey of the evolution of Islam in pre-Mongol Iran. Rather the hope was to shed light on the motivation of some of the religious movements of the time which may help bring about a better understanding of the major lines of their development in conflict and resolution.

My thanks are due to Ehsan Yarshater without whose initiative, encouragement, and support the lectures would not have been written and published.

Mazdakism and the Khurramiyya

Islam required from its early Persian converts an almost total break with their own religious traditions. Unlike Judaism and Christianity, whose prophetic origins were acknowledged by Islam, Zoroastrianism, even though it gained a similar legal status as the "book religions" tolerated by the Qur'an, was unequivocally condemned as a false religion. Its founder was a pseudo-prophet without any trace of divine authority. Muslims thus had no incentive to examine the Zoroastrian heritage for elements of religious value as they might search Jewish and Christian scripture and tradition. Zoroastrianism was equally negative in its attitude toward Islam. Put on the defensive by the victorious new religion, it strove to preserve its religious identity and heritage from foreign contamination. There was nothing to be learned from Islam.

In spite of this uncompromising antagonism between the two faiths, the eighth and ninth centuries witnessed a number of popular revolutionary movements in Iran which overtly mixed Persian and Islamic religious beliefs and motives. The generic name most often applied to these movements in the sources is Khurramdīniyya or Khurramiyya. The name, itself Persian, clearly refers to the Iranian component of their religion. This is generally identified by the Muslim heresiographers as the teaching of Mazdak, the religious and social revolutionary of the age of the Sassanian Kavādh (488–531). The identity of the Khurramiyya in early Islamic times with the remnants of the movement backing Mazdak is generally recognized by modern scholarship, even though the name Khurramdīn cannot definitely be traced back to pre-Islamic origins.[1]

More problematic is the nature of the religious foundation of the Mazdakite movement, especially before the impact of Islam on it. Our sources for Mazdakite beliefs and practices are almost exclusively Islamic, and much of their reports relates to the neo-Mazdakite sects which caught the eye of the Muslim authors after their entanglement with Islamic heresies. The most detailed account of the teaching of Mazdak himself, that of the late heresiographer al-Shahrastānī,[2] stands apart from the other reports, and its sources are unknown. It

1. On the relationship between Mazdakism and the Khurramiyya see in general the article "Khurramiyya" in *E.I.*, 2nd ed., and E. Yarshater, chapter on Mazdakism in *Cambridge History of Iran,* III, pp. 991–1024.

2. Al-Shahrastānī, *al-Milal wa l-niḥal,* pp. 192–194.

has often been assumed that al-Shahrastānī throughout this account quoted Abū ʿĪsā al-Warrāq, a well-known ninth-century authority on dualist religions whom he mentions at its beginning, but this has proved to be erroneous.[3]

The questions raised by the reports of the sources and the results of modern research on the religious nature of Mazdakism cannot be dealt with here in detail. Only a few relevant points may be noted. Mazdak does not appear as the founder of the movement supporting him. To what extent he himself transformed or modified the religious and social teaching of his followers is uncertain. In respect to the essential character of the religion, A. Christensen, who published his fundamental monograph on Mazdakism in 1925, described it as an off-shoot from Manichaeism.[4] More recent studies rather suggest that Mazdakism, though certainly influenced by Manichaeism, was a Zoroastrian reform movement.[5] The Mazdakites claimed to represent the true religion of Zoroaster rather than a new faith. Although they were critical of established Mazdakism, they did not endeavor to destroy the basic structure of the Zoroastrian Church or to leave it. They thus could be described as a Low Church, representing popular religious and social sentiments, in relation to the High Church of orthodox Zoroastrianism, which represented the conservative interests of the aristocracy. The arguments in favor of this view are strong. It is also in agreement with what is known about the character of the Khurramiyya in the time of Islam. The Khurramiyya represented Persian national sentiments looking forward to a restoration of Persian sovereign rule in contrast to the universalist religious tendencies of Manichaeism.

Early Mazdakism, however, was evidently more receptive to foreign influences than the Zoroastrian High Church. Its very origins may well be connected with a syncretistic opening to the influence of other religions, in particular Manichaeism. Syncretism, receptivity to external influence, could, on the other hand, easily endanger doctrinal uniformity. There is no lack of evidence for divergence and religious diversity within Mazdakism. The different names given locally to the neo-Mazdakite and Khurramī sects must have often covered religious differences although the accounts do not always clearly identify them.

3. See "Abū ʿĪsā al-Warrāq über die Bardesaniten, Marcioniten und Kantäer," p. 221, n. 36.

4. A Christensen, *Le Régne du roi Kawādh I et le communisme mazdakite*, pp. 98ff.

5. O. Klíma, *Mazdak: Geschichte einer sozialen Bewegung im sassanidischen Persien*, pp. 204ff.; Yarshater, pp. 995–998.

It is not unlikely that there was much more diversity in the Zoroastrian Low Church from which the followers of Mazdak mostly came than can be established from the meager sources, just as later the followers of Abū Muslim al-Khurāsānī, figurehead of the neo-Mazdakite movement, were drawn from diverse religious backgrounds.

The situation may be illustrated by the case of a little-known religious sect of Mesopotamian origin related to the baptist Mandaeans: the Kantaeans or, probably more correct, Kanthaeans. We are informed about the origins of this sect only by the Nestorian Theodore Bar Konai writing in Syriac in 791–792.[6] According to him the sect was founded, or rather reformed, by the Babylonian Baṭṭai who introduced traditional Persian fire worship among the sectarians and assumed the Persian name Yazdānī, during the reign of the Sassanian Peroz (459–487) because of the latter's ban of all religions aside from Zoroastrianism. Already before, Baṭṭai had adopted and adapted some Manichaean texts and mystery rites. Bar Konai further describes the gnostic doctrine of the Kanthaeans in some detail.

Baṭṭai Yazdānī thus was active only a generation before Mazdak in the very region from which the latter is mostly assumed to have come. The name of Mazdak's hometown mentioned by al-Ṭabarī has been identified by Christensen with Mādharāyā in southern Babylonia.[7] It is thus almost certain that he was at least acquainted with the teaching of Baṭṭai. On this account, the possibility of an influence of Kanthaean gnosticism on Mazdak has been noted in passing by O. Klíma.[8]

Until recently, however, Bar Konai's account was practically the only source on the sect, and its very existence has been questioned. H. H. Schaeder has argued in a special article on the subject that the Syriac name Kantayē was a corruption of Kūthayē, an abusive name applied by the Jews to the Samaritans, and was erroneously transferred by Christian heresiographers to the Mandaeans. Schaeder considered Bar Konai's account of the history of the Kanthaeans in its entirety as a concoction of the Syriac Christian heresiography.[9]

The existence of the Kanthaean sect and its survival at least until the early ʿAbbasid age are now corroborated by Islamic Arabic sources.[10] Their mention of it has long been overlooked since its name

6. Bar Konai's account of the Kanthaeans was first analyzed by H. Pognon, *Inscriptions Mandaïtes des Coupes de Khouabir.*

7. Christensen, p. 100.

8. Klíma, pp. 159, 185.

9. H. H. Schaeder, "Die Kantäer," in *WO,* I, pp. 288–298.

10. "Abū ʿĪsā al-Warrāq," pp. 221–224.

appears in the published Arabic sources as Kaynāniyya or Kīnāniyya and in al-Shahrastānī's account as Kaynawiyya or Kīnawiyya. This corruption of the name could easily occur in the Arabic script since it required merely a change of dots which were frequently omitted in early Arabic writing. It is likely that the later Arabic heresiographers, and in particular al-Shahrastānī, no longer knew the correct name and read it in its corrupted form. The identity of the sect mentioned by the Muslim authors with the Kantayē of the Christian heresiographers is definitely proved by a still unedited quotation of Abū ʿĪsā al-Warrāq who, like Bar Konai, derives the name of the sect from that of their temple, Kantā or Kanthā. This reading is in the Syriac script, unlike the Arabic, certain, except for the alternative of *t* and *th* which is not distinguishable in it. The Arabic manuscript tradition clearly favors the reading of *th* so that the word should be read Kanthā. It is certainly, as suggested already by H. Pognon,[11] derived from the root *k-n-n,* related in meaning to the Arabic *kann* or *kinn,* which means abode, shelter, or house, with the feminine ending.

The Muslim heresiographers regularly report the doctrine of the Kanthaeans that the world was constituted out of three basic elements, fire, earth, and water. Their particular mention of this cosmological doctrine, which is not reported by Bar Konai, indicates that they knew about the sect chiefly through its participation in debates about cosmology with representatives of other religions and schools which were held most likely in the circle of the Barmakids. The sect thus evidently preserved an identity until early ʿAbbasid times and seems to have disintegrated soon afterwards. The Islamic sources say nothing about its distribution. However, al-Shahrastānī, who offers the most detailed Islamic account, which, like his report on Mazdak, is based on an unknown early ʿAbbasid source, speaks of at least three branches of the sect. One of them, called the Ṣiyāmiyya, laid great stress on ascetic practices and abstention from sexual intercourse and the slaughter of animals. Another branch believed in the transmigration of souls.[12] This account gives the impression that the sect, after its adoption of fire worship, expanded far beyond its original southern Babylonian home into Iranian territory.

How is this apparent expansion of the Persianized Mesopotamian sect related to Mazdakism? Was it an unrelated development and a mere accident that both reformers originated in the same region or

11. Pognon, p. 228, n. 2.
12. Al-Shahrastānī, pp. 196–197.

was Mazdak's religious teaching a further development of that of Baṭṭai Yazdānī and the spread of the sect in Iran partly a result of Mazdak's activity? It may not be possible to answer these questions definitively unless some further relevant sources are discovered. None of the sources presently available establishes any link between the Kanthaeans and Mazdakism.

There are, however, notable similarities between the religious doctrines of the Kanthaeans and of Mazdak especially as reported by al-Shahrastānī. The Kanthaeans and Mazdak both affirmed, in spite of their essential dualism, the existence of three original elements, fire, earth, and water. According to Bar Konai, Baṭṭai taught that the Lord God was assisted by seven good forces produced by His seven Words and by another twelve. They were opposed by seven demons and, presumably twelve, devils representing evil.[13] Mazdak, according to al-Shahrastānī's account, affirmed that God was attended by four forces ruling the world who were assisted by seven ministers (*wuzarāʾ*) and twelve spiritual beings (*rūḥāniyyūn*). God, the King of the Higher World, is further described as ruling with the letters (*ḥurūf*) whose total constituted the Greatest Name (*al-ism al-aʿẓam*). These letters may well be identical with the seven ministers given their instrumentality in ruling the world. The four powers attending God corresponded to four dignitaries attending Chosroes on earth and four powers of evil.[14] Al-Shahrastānī's summary account does not mention similar correspondences for the seven and the twelve. In view of the obvious parallelism of the system, however, it must seem likely that there were numerical counterparts on earth and among the forces of evil.

There is, moreover, a remarkable coincidence between the divisions of the Kanthaean sect into branches described by al-Shahrastānī and what is known about the various currents in the Mazdakiyya and Khurramiyya in early Islamic times. Mazdak is usually described by the hostile sources as a permissive libertinist, and the Khurramdīniyya mostly took, as their name implies, a positive attitude to the joys and pleasures of life. However, the presence of a distinctive current of asceticism among them, similar to the Ṣiyāmiyya among the Kanthaeans, is also well attested.[15] Belief in the transmigration of souls is known to have been widespread among the Khurramiyya, as in the third division of al-Shahrastānī's Kanthawiyya, though it is not attested for either Mazdak or Baṭṭai. In view of these striking similarities, the

13. Pognon, p. 223.
14. Al-Shahrastānī, p. 193.
15. See Yarshater, p. 1012.

question may well be asked whether al-Shahrastānī's Kanthawiyya are not identical with some of the Mazdakiyya and Khurramiyya mentioned in the other sources, especially in western Iran.

Yet even if Mazdak stood in his religious teaching close to the Kanthaeans and these constituted a basic element in his following, it is evident that, as a man of action and practical reformer rather than a religious teacher, his following was more broadly based and included other religious groups, especially in northwestern Iran and Transoxania. Al-Shahrastānī mentions among the Mazdakite sects a Māhāniyya and locates them in Transoxania.[16] The Māhāniyya are described by other heresiographers as a dualist sect closely related to the Marcionites. According to Abū ʿĪsā al-Warrāq, "They maintained churches and crosses and inclined to Christianity." They considered Christ the Adjuster *(muʿaddil),* i.e., the Third Being between Light and Darkness who is the Creator of the World. They rejected the asceticism of the Marcionites with their prohibition of marriage and eating of meat. According to al-Warrāq it was also reported of them that they affirmed the three basic elements. These may well be the three elements of the Kanthaeans and Mazdak, fire, earth, and water. The sect was most likely an offshoot from the Marcionite church which is known to have survived in Transoxania at least until the tenth century. There is evidence that Marcionism in eastern Iran came under strong dualist influence, although Abū ʿĪsā al-Warrāq's account shows that a more authentic tradition of Marcion's teaching also survived.[17] The Māhāniyya may have been transformed more specifically by Mazdakite teaching.[18]

The Mazdakiyya with whom the Muslims became acquainted after the conquest of Iran thus were certainly not a single sect with uniform religious beliefs and practices and a common leadership. Rather they appear as a conglomorate of sects and currents basically characterized by a cosmic dualism and a gnostic syncretism and loosely held together by an allegiance to the revolutionary movement of Mazdak and at least nominal commitment to an ideal Zoroastrian state church, though

16. Al-Shahrastānī, p. 193. For the following see also "Abū ʿĪsā al-Warrāq," pp. 217, 220.

17. "Abū ʿĪsā al-Warrāq," pp. 215–220.

18. It is to be noted that Baṭṭai, according to Bar Konai, in his syncretism also borrowed from the Christians the sign of the cross which "he threw on the left shoulder of his followers." His followers said that the cross was the secret of the boundary between the Father of Greatness, the High God in Baṭṭai's doctrine, and the lower world. Pognon, p. 222. According to al-Warrāq, some people counted the Kanthaeans among the Christians. Christian elements appear, however, marginal in the Kanthaean system.

not to its established hierarchy. Their syncretistic outlook made them naturally more receptive to foreign religious influences than the dogmatically more uniform and institutionally unified Zoroastrian High Church. Yet it required a movement of a similar revolutionary and syncretistic nature to bring about the fusion of Iranian dualist and Islamic elements apparent in the Khurramiyya. Such a movement arose in the Kaysāniyya, the radical Shiʿite, messianic movement which initially backed the imamate of ʿAlī's son Muḥammad b. al-Ḥanafiyya and later gave rise to the ʿAbbasid revolutionary movement.

The beginnings of the involvement of the Khurramiyya with the Kaysāniyya can probably be dated to the time of Abū Hāshim, the son of Muḥammad b. al-Ḥanafiyya, who, after the latter's death in 81/700 actively asserted his leadership of the movement that had looked to his father as their imam and set up a secret missionary organization to gain support for his cause, especially in Iraq and Iran. Abū Hāshim is accused of having espoused extremist Shiʿite doctrines. By the time of his death around 98/717–718 his party, known as the Hāshimiyya, was already widespread. That some of his followers had been recruited among the Khurramiyya is indicated by the prominent role they soon began to play in both major branches into which the Hāshimiyya split. Among the branch supporting ʿAbd Allāh b. Muʿāwiya, a great-grandson of ʿAlī's brother Jaʿfar, an extremist Shiʿite, gnostic doctrine was taught by a certain ʿAbd Allāh b. al-Ḥarb (or al-Ḥārith), who is described as the son of a *zindīq,* i.e., a dualist heretic, from al-Madāʾin. It comprised, besides the exaltation of the imams as prophets, angels, and even as divine, belief in the preexistence of the souls as shadows *(aẓilla),* in the transmigration of souls, cyclical return to this world, and the denial of the resurrection. His teaching was, according to the heresiographers, the foundation of the doctrine adopted and transmitted by the Kufan extremist Shiʿite *ghulāt* groups which throve at the fringe of the Imāmī Shīʿa supporting the Ḥusaynid imams. This is fully substantiated by the extant remnants of the *ghulāt* literature, in particular the *Kitāb al-Haft wa l-aẓilla* preserved by the Nuṣayrīs.[19] According to the heresiographers, ʿAbd Allāh b. Ḥarb's doctrine also spread among the factions of the Khurramdīniyya,[20] evidently in Mesopotamia and western Iran where they backed ʿAbd Allāh b. Muʿāwiya.

19. H. Halm, "Das 'Buch der Schatten': Die Mufaḍḍal-Tradition der Ġulāt und die Ursprünge des Nuṣairiertums," in *Der Islam* LV, pp. 219–1266, LVIII, pp. 15–86; see esp. LVIII, pp. 16ff.

20. Al-Nawbakhtī, *Firaq al-shīʿa,* p. 36; Saʿd b. ʿAbd Allāh, *al-Maqālāt wa l-firaq,* p. 44.

In the other branch of the Hāshimiyya, which supported the imamate of the ʿAbbasid Muḥammad b. ʿAlī, the *dāʿī* nicknamed Khidāsh,[21] who was active in the regions of Nishapur and Marw around 111–118/729–736 is accused of having taught the religion of the Khurramiyya and allowed sexual promiscuity. Khidāsh was repudiated by the ʿAbbasid imam and killed, probably at his instigation. According to pseudo-Nāshiʾ, who identifies the Khurramiyya of Khurasan with the Khidāshiyya, the partisans of Khidāsh, they later held that the imamate had been forfeited by Muḥammad b. ʿAlī and had passed to Khidāsh whose death they denied.[22]

The widest allegiance among the Khurramiyya all over Iran and Transoxania was, however, gained by Abū Muslim al-Khurāsānī. The heresiographers indeed often identify the Khurramiyya with the Abū Muslimiyya or Muslimiyya who recognized Abū Muslim as their imam and a prophet or an incarnation of the divine spirit. The widespread and fervent popular backing of Abū Muslim in Iran which is reflected in this religious allegiance of the Khurramiyya is a significant factor in the success of the ʿAbbasid revolution and must be stressed in view of recent interpretations which see the revolution as essentially Arab. While the revolutionary army was led by Khurasanian Arabs, it had the backing of the Persian populace, Muslim and non-Muslim. The Umayyad armies might not have collapsed so quickly if they had not been operating in enemy country.

The watershed between the ʿAbbasid movement and the Khurramiyya was reached with the murder of Abū Muslim by the caliph al-Manṣūr in 137/753. The Khurasanian Muslims, Arabs and Persians, remained loyal for the most part to the house of the ʿAbbasids. The Khurramiyya reaffirmed and strengthened their religious commitment to Abū Muslim who had come to symbolize Persian self-assertion against Arab domination and ʿAbbasid perfidy. Revolts in his name broke out in various regions of Iran. Some of his followers denied his death and expected his return. Others held that the imamate had passed to his daughter Fāṭima. Later her son, named Muṭahhar or Gōhar, was recognized as the imam and the *kūdak-i dānā,* the omniscient child, who would reappear as the Mahdī. Some of the Khur-

21. See on him Sharon, "Khidāsh," in *E.I.*, 2nd ed., and *Black Banners from the East,* pp. 165–173, 180–186. Sharon's argument that Khidāsh was repudiated by the ʿAbbasids because he furthered the ʿAlid cause is not convincing.

22. Al-Nāshiʾ, *Masāʾil al-imāma,* ed. J. van Ess, pp. 32–135. Concerning the authorship of the text see "Frühe Muʿtazilitische Häresiographie: das *Kitāb al-Uṣūl* des Ǧaʿfar b. Ḥarb?"

ramiyya claimed, according to al-Dīnawarī,[23] that Bābak, the great Khurramī rebel, was a son of this Muṭahhar.

There is no need to pursue the history of the Khurramiyya and their revolts further here. It has been thoroughly investigated and described by H. Sadighi in his well-known book *Les Mouvements religieux iraniens au IIe et IIIe siècle de l'hégire* and by others after him. In conclusion, attention may rather be drawn to a report on a Khurramī group which has so far escaped proper notice.[24] It is one of the latest definite reports on the sectarians and comes from the pen of a Nizārī Ismaᶜīlī chronicler, Dehkhodā ᶜAbd al-Malik b. ᶜAlī. He is perhaps identical with the Dehkhodā ᶜAbd al-Malik Fashandī who was appointed commander of the fortress of Maymūndiz in Rabīᶜ I 520/April 1126.[25] The original of the report is lost but two variant versions of it are contained in Rashīd al-Dīn's *Jāmiᶜ al-tawārīkh* and the *Zubdat al-tawārīkh* of Abu l-Qāsim Kāshānī.

Under the year 536/1141–1142 Dehkhodā ᶜAbd al-Malik notes that a group of Mazdakites—he does not use the term Khurramiyya though the identity is evident—who had earlier joined the Ismāᶜīlī *daᶜwa* revealed their abominable secret beliefs. The sectarians called themselves Pārsīs (Pārsiyān). The name, which was also used for the Zoroastrians, especially in India, is not attested elsewhere for the Khurramiyya. Its adoption by them evidently reflected their attachment to the Persian religion and national traditions.

The sectarians apparently lived in or came from Adharbayjan and thus were most likely remnants of the Khurramī followers of Bābak.[26] Some decades before, they had nominally accepted Ismaᶜilism. This was, the Ismaᶜīlī chronicler comments, in accordance with their usual practice. Whenever a faith or religious doctrine became dominant, they would pretend to back it while keeping their true beliefs concealed. Thus when they saw the Ismāᶜīlīs becoming strong they said: "This is the true faith, we accept it." Sayyidnā Ḥasan-i Ṣabbāḥ, then

23. Al-Dīnawarī, *al-Akhbār al-ṭiwāl,* p. 397. Al-Dīnawarī himself accepts this descent of Bābak.

24. Rashīd al-Dīn, *Jāmiᶜ al-tawārīkh: qismat-i Ismāᶜīliyya,* ed. M. T. Dānishpazhūh and M. Mudarresī, pp. 149–163; Kāshānī, *Tārīkh-i Ismāᶜīliyya,* ed. M. T. Dānishpazhūh, pp. 171–174. The report was summarily noted by M. G. S. Hodgson, *The Order of Assassins,* pp. 71–72. Hodgson missed its significance suggesting that the group were perhaps merely some popular heretics within the Ismāᶜīlī community. This is untenable in view of the specific doctrines ascribed to them.

25. Rashīd al-Dīn, p. 138.

26. According to the version of Rashīd al-Dīn (p. 151), the weaver Budayl preached to the Pārsiyān in Adharbayjan. In the version of Kāshānī, Adharbayjan is not mentioned.

chief of the Nizārīs, sent Dehkhodā Kaykhosrow, who had formerly belonged to them, to teach them the Ismāʿīlī faith. When Kaykhosrow died in Muḥarram 513/April–May 1119, his sons Abu l-ʿAlāʾ and Yūsuf took his place as their leaders. The sons were, however, thirsty for money and worldly prestige and forgot their faith. Ḥasan-i Ṣabbāḥ exhorted and warned them, but to no avail. After Ḥasan-i Ṣabbāḥ's death (518/1124) a weaver named Budayl arose among them and told them: "The truth is with the Pārsīs; the Ismāʿīlīs are people clinging to the exterior of religion (*mardom-e ẓāherī and*). The esoteric truth is that Abu l-ʿAlāʾ and Yūsuf are now in the position of Muḥammad and ʿAlī. Muḥammad, ʿAlī, and Salmān were all three God; for He appears at one time in a single person, at another in two, and at another in three persons. The law of the *sharīʿa* is only for those adhering to the exterior of religion. There is no reality to what is declared lawful or forbidden in religion. Prayer and fasting must therefore be abandoned." Budayl further told them that women were the water of the house which was licit for every thirsty man to drink. Dowry and marriage contract had no meaning. Daughters were lawful for their fathers and brothers. Thus they considered all forbidden things licit. They also said that heaven and hell were on earth and that every one who recognized the divinity of Abu l-ʿAlāʾ and Yūsuf would return to earth in human shape, while those failing to do so would return in the shape of wild beasts.

When this teaching became known, the Ismāʿīlīs seized some of the heretics and forced them through torture to confess. Abu l-ʿAlāʾ and Yūsuf then were apprehended (9 Rabīʿ II 537/31 October 1142) and pressed to recant but they resisted. Both were put to death and burned. Within a year all their followers were also killed.

The Ismāʿīlī author goes on to give some further details about the beliefs of these deluded sectarians as he sees them. They held that no one is allowed to harm any animal or plant, to such a degree that no pale should be hammered into the ground lest the earth suffer pain. It was improper to have two wives as harm would accrue to both of them. Nor was repudiation (*ṭalāq*) of the wife or purchase of any slave allowed. There were indeed five sins (though only four are mentioned in the text) whose perpetrator would not escape hell: To shed blood unjustly, to have two wives at a time, to establish ties with a religious opponent, and to harm men by either tongue or limbs. The sectarians interpreted the resurrection and the hereafter in the light of their doctrine of metempsychosis. Thus they said that paradise consists in (being reborn in) human shape, though the cosmic paradise (*behesht-*

e garzamān) is in heaven. The latter phrase may indicate that they believed in an eventual ingathering of the souls of the saved in a heavenly paradise. This description of their religion agrees largely with information about the Khurramiyya from other sources and, with allowance for some polemical exaggeration, probably represents it faithfully.

The account then deals with their belief concerning "dissociation and loyalty" *(tabarrā wa-tawallā),* i.e., the imamate, a subject obviously of central importance for the Ismāᶜīlīs. The sectarians held that the Great Kings of the Persians since Jamshīd had been rightful imams. From them the imamate had passed to Muḥammad and ᶜAlī, then to Muḥammad b. al-Ḥanafiyya, from him to the ᶜAbbāsid Ibrāhīm b. Muḥammad, and then to Abū Muslim Marwazī and to his grandson Gōhar. The Ismāᶜīlī author naturally pours scorn on this, from his Ismāᶜīlī point of view most extraordinary, line of imams. How, he asks, could the Persian Kings and then Muḥammad and ᶜAlī all have been rightful imams when there was total opposition and much bloodshed between them? How could there be any agreement between them and both be saying the truth? How could Muḥammad b. al-Ḥanafiyya, even if he was a son of ᶜAlī, be the imam in the presence of Ḥasan and Ḥusayn, the darlings of the Prophet? And if we accepted that he was the imam, how could the imamate have passed from him to the ᶜAbbāsid Ibrāhīm and, even more absurdly, from the latter to Abū Muslim? And Gōhar to whom it allegedly then passed has been hidden for more than five hundred years,[27] so that no one has had access to their imam. Muḥammad and ᶜAlī would have considered anyone affirming such a fraud an infidel.

This report and the polemic of the Ismāᶜīlī author highlight both the gulf between the Khurramī and Ismāᶜīlī conception of the imamate and the persistent commitment of the Khurramiyya to Persian religious and national tradition. In contrast to the line of Qurʾanic prophets and their successors through which the Ismāᶜīlīs traced the pre-Islamic imamate, the Khurramiyya considered the Persian kings as their imams. Nothing is said about their attitude to the prophets recognized by Islam. The legitimate dominance of Arab Islam lasted only a short time. Already after the death of ᶜAlī the imamate passed to leaders of the oppressed, Muḥammad b. al-Ḥanafiyya and the ᶜAbbasid Ibrāhīm b. Muḥammad, against the illegitimate caliphs.

27. It is not clear whether this number is an erroneous exaggeration of the Ismāᶜīlī author or the result of a later adjustment of a copyist.

With Abū Muslim the imamate returned to the Persians. Although his heroic effort to break the Arab domination and restore justice eventually ended in failure because of the perfidy of the caliph al-Manṣūr, his grandson would complete his work and restore the Persian religion and domination as the Mahdī. Islam thus was nothing but a brief interlude in the religious tradition of Iran.[28]

28. There is a final charge made by the Ismāʿīlī author against the heretics whose significance is more obscure. According to him, it was their doctrine that every one who possesses wealth and prestige will be rewarded. On that basis, he comments, prophets and saints will be punished, while all evil men and criminals will be rewarded. The point is evidently connected with the accusation made earlier against Abu l-ʿAlāʾ and Yūsuf that they aspired to wealth and power forgetting their Ismāʿīlī faith and were reprimanded for this by Ḥasan-i Ṣabbāḥ. It is likely that they did not deliver as large a share of their economic gains to the imam and his representative, Ḥasan-i Ṣabbāḥ, as Ismāʿīlīs were expected to do. But here their striving for wealth and power is given a religious motivation. The Khurramiyya were noted for their positive attitude to the joys of life which presumably included the enjoyment of wealth and prestige. But did they go so far as to develop a Calvinist belief that worldly success was the sign of divine favor and reward in the hereafter?

The Murjiʾa and Sunnite Traditionalism

Islam was introduced in Iran by conquest. The Muslim Arab invaders, however, primarily sought to establish their domination in the name of Islam over the conquered territories and to reduce the people to subjects of the Islamic state. It was not their aim to convert the indigenous non-Muslims to Islam by force. At times it must even have seemed as if they wished to discourage conversion. Arab national interest could in this respect converge to some extent with conservative, rigorist Islamic motives. Arab interest, firmly represented by the Umayyad caliphate, pressed for maintenance of Arab rule in the conquered lands and was wary of uncontrolled mass conversion which would naturally encourage claims to equality and a share of the power in the name of Islam and would threaten the tax base of the state resting on the non-Muslim subjects. Conservative Muslim sentiment was equally apprehensive about the potential dilution of the purity of Islam by a massive influx of nominal converts.

Under these circumstances, conversion to Islam in the early time normally meant not only acceptance of the new faith but also Arabization, integration into Arab society. The converts adopted Arabic names and learned Arabic, the language of the Qurʾan and Islamic worship, sometimes to a high level of literary refinement. They were attached as clients, *mawālī,* to an Arab lord or to a clan. *Mawālī* indeed became the common term for the non-Arab Muslims. While the status of clients gave them a place in Arab society, it also affirmed their rank at the bottom of it. The temptation to conceal non-Arab origin and to claim outright Arab descent was strong. Many *mawālī,* as is well known, succumbed to it.

While the Arab ruling class generally did not favor mass conversion to Islam, it naturally encouraged those non-Arabs with whom it had close personal contact to accept its faith and conform with its practices and standards. Personal slaves, servants, tenants, retainers and even tradesmen were no doubt often under some pressure, though not legally obliged, to become Muslims. Conversions in the early times thus most commonly took place in the immediate vicinity of the Arab settlements. They were most substantial in the areas with the largest Arab garrisons. In Iran that meant in Khurasan, especially in the region of Marw. In Khurasan Iranian *mawālī* are also mentioned from the early time as serving in the Muslim army. The Arab lords went usually to war with their Iranian retainers. The clients fought on foot only, however, while their masters were horsemen. This led soon to the establishment of separate regiments composed only of *mawālī*, even under the command of non-Arabs. Their leaders gained considerable prestige and acted at times as power brokers between opposing factions. They assisted the Arabs in their wars against non-Muslims, Turks and Iranian Soghdians, but generally refused to get involved in the intertribal Arab feuds. There could be no question about their essential loyalty to official Islam, to their Arab masters, and to the Umayyad regime.

This pattern of controlled conversion broke down in Transoxania. The number of Arab settlers there was small and restricted to the major towns. Large groups of the indigenous population, in particular Soghdians, were prepared to accept Islam together with their princes. Many of them had previously been allied with the Muslims and had fought at their side against the enemies of Islam. The Umayyad administration, however, resisted their claims to be Muslims and in particular rejected their demands that they be exempted from the tribute *(jizya)* imposed on them as non-Muslims.

The cause of these mass converts to Islam was taken up by the religious movement known as the Murjiʾa.[1] The movement was not initially concerned with the status and rights of the *mawālī* in Central Asia. It originated in the aftermath of the great Kufan Shiʿite revolt led by al-Mukhtār in favor of Muḥammad b. al-Ḥanafiyya and advocated a return to the unity among the Muslims by avoiding all extreme partisan views concerning the caliphate. Its basic contention was that judgment of the conduct of ʿUthmān and ʿAlī should be deferred to God, while the caliphate of Abū Bakr and ʿUmar, under whom concord had prevailed among the Muslims, deserved unconditional praise and emulation. The early Murjiʾa thus distanced themselves from the extreme Shīʿa repudiating the caliphs preceding ʿAlī, the Khārijites condemning both ʿUthmān and ʿAlī, and the ʿUthmāniyya repudiating ʿAlī which represented the official Umayyad position. They were at first mainly concentrated in Kufa, where they constituted the major non-Shiʿite current, and, on a smaller scale, in Basra. Although they did not in principle oppose the Umayyad caliphate and in general held that Muslims should not fight other Muslims except in self-defense, they were drawn into the anti-Umayyad rebellions of ʿAbd al-Raḥmān b. al-Ashʿath and of Yazīd b. al-Muhallab. There was ob-

1. For the following see in general, "The Early Murjiʾa in Khurāsān and Transoxania and the Spread of Ḥanafism."

viously a certain tension between their affirmation that no one adhering to the true religion should be denied his status as a faithful Muslim on account of any wrongdoing and their espousal of the duty of every Muslim to speak out against injustice. The importance of this duty in their eyes was reflected in the name they applied to themselves: People of Justice and the Sunna *(ahl al-ʿadl wa l-sunna)*.[2]

The engagement of the Murjiʾa on behalf of the new converts to Islam in Transoxania for their equality as Muslims and their exemption from the *jizya* was evidently an aspect of their struggle for justice under Islam. Doctrinally it was mainly based, however, on their thesis that faith (*īmān*) consists in mere belief and confession of Islam to the exclusion of works, i.e., the performance of the ritual and legal obligations of Islam. This meant that the legal status of a Muslim and of a true believer *(muʾmin)* could not be denied to these converts on the pretext that they ignored or failed to perform some of the essential duties of the Muslim. The definition of faith as excluding works had previously been only a secondary point in Murjiʾite doctrine deriving from their opposition to the excommunication of Muslims for wrongdoing, real or imagined, and may not have been part of their earliest teaching. It now took on an added practical significance and was later generally treated by the heresiographers as the most fundamental dogma of the Murjiʾa. Their early central thesis concerning the first four caliphs gradually lost all interest as it was close enough to the later common Sunnite doctrine to be ignored.

The involvement of the Murjiʾa in the struggle for the rights of the *mawālī* and in the mass conversions in the east is first mentioned under the Umayyad caliph ʿUmar II. The latter, as is well known, strongly favored conversion to Islam and was generally sympathetic to the cause of the Murjiʾa. Al-Ṭabarī reports under the year 100/718–719 that a client, who is identified as either Abu l-Ṣaydāʾ Ṣāliḥ b. Ṭarīf al-Ḍabbī or Saʿīd al-Naḥwī, complained before the caliph that 20,000 *mawālī* participated in eastern military campaigns without a stipend and a like number of new converts were forced to pay tribute. ʿUmar now instructed the governor of Khurasan, al-Jarrāḥ b. ʿAbd Allāh, to exempt all those praying in the direction of Mekka from the *jizya*. As a result the masses hastened to accept Islam. Al-Jarrāḥ was advised by his officials that the people were flocking to Islam only in order to escape the *jizya* and that he should test them by requiring circumcision

2. J. Schacht, "An Early Murciʾite Treatise: The Kitāb al-ʿĀlim wal-Mutaʿallim," in *Oriens* XVII, p. 102; W. Madelung, *Der Imam al-Qāsim ibn Ibrāhīm*, p. 235.

of the converts. Al-Jarrāḥ referred this suggestion to the caliph who wrote back: "God sent Muḥammad as a summoner, not as a circumciser." Al-Jarrāḥ was replaced by a governor more in line with ʿUmar's political views.

ʿUmar's policies of encouraging conversion evidently did not remain in force for long after his death. Under the year 110/728–729 al-Ṭabarī reports that the governor of Khurasan, Ashras b. ʿAbd Allāh, asked his advisers to name a pious and virtuous man whom he would send to Transoxania to summon the people to Islam. They suggested Abu l-Ṣaydāʾ and, since he was not skilled in Persian, he was given a companion. Abu l-Ṣaydāʾ stipulated that whoever would convert to Islam should be exempted from paying the *jizya,* and the governor agreed. The people of the region of Samarqand flocked in large numbers to join Islam as Abu l-Ṣaydāʾ promised them exemption from the *jizya.* Ghūrak, the native prince responsible to the Muslims for the tribute of the Soghdians, complained to Ashras about the erosion of the tax-paying community. Ashras now wrote Ibn Abi l-ʿAmarraṭa, the governor of Samarqand: "The power of the Muslims rests in the tribute. I have learned that the Soghdians and their likes have not become Muslims out of a desire (for Islam). They have joined Islam merely in order to avoid the *jizya.* Examine therefore whoever has been circumcised, performs the ritual obligations *(farāʾiḍ),* whose Islam is unimpeachable, and who is able to recite a sura of the Qurʾan. Exempt him from his tribute."

This restrictive interpretation of Islam evidently still did not bring the desired results. Ashras took away Ibn al-ʿAmarraṭa's authority over taxation and put an independent official in charge. When Abu l-Ṣaydāʾ objected to the latter's taking *jizya* from the converts, he reported to Ashras that the people had (truly) become Muslims and built mosques. Now the Dehqāns of Bukhara came to Ashras saying: "From whom will you take the tribute since all the people have become Arabs?" Ashras instructed the tax official to reimpose the tribute on all those from whom it had previously been taken. As the *jizya* was demanded again from the Muslim converts, some 7,000 Soghdians seceded and assembled at a place seven *farsakh*s from Samarqand. Abu l-Ṣaydāʾ and a group of his associates joined them there in protest. Among them was the poet Thābit Quṭna, a prominent champion of the faith against the infidels and author of a well-known poem in which he expounded and defended the religious doctrine of the Murjiʾa. A new governor of Samarqand sent by Ashras succeeded in luring Abu l-Ṣaydāʾ and Thābit Quṭna to join him and imprisoned them. The rebellion of the Soghdians soon collapsed, the leaders were arrested and sent to Marw, and the tribute was pressed out of the people with utmost ruthlessness. This led to their defection from Islam and an alliance with the infidel Turks, which endangered the Arab position in all of Transoxania. In the ensuing war Thābit Quṭna, who had been released from prison, was killed.

Six years later, in 116/734, the great Murjiʾite revolt under al-Ḥārith b. Surayj erupted. Al-Ḥārith is first mentioned as distinguishing himself for his bravery in the campaign in which Thābit Quṭna was killed. His revolt lasted, with some interruptions, until his death in 128/746. Most of his initial support came from the regions of Lower Ṭukhāristān, Jūzjān, Fāryāb, Ṭāliqān, and Balkh. When he later was pushed out of the Muslim territories, he was forced, however, to ally himself with the Khāqān of the Türgesh and other infidel chiefs. Among his most intimate and active supporters were several of the former associates of Abu l-Ṣaydāʾ, like Rabīʿ b. ʿImrān al-Taymī, Bishr b. Jurmūz al-Ḍabbī, Abū Fāṭima al-Azdī, and al-Qāsim al-Shaybānī, who had backed the Soghdian converts in their resistance against their continued subjection to the *jizya*. Eventually the theologian Jahm b. Ṣafwān became the religious spokesman of the rebel movement. Jahm was later commonly condemned by Muslims of almost all shades of opinion as one of the arch-heretics of Islam on account of the radicalism of some of his views. Traditionalists denigrated his memory in particular as one of the authors of the doctrine of the created nature of the Qurʾan. He also upheld an extreme Murjiʾite position defining faith as mere belief in the heart irrespective of verbal affirmation *(iqrār)* stipulated by the more moderate Murjiʾa.

In his political program, al-Ḥārith was also distinctly more radical than the mainstream of the Murjiʾa. Raising the popular call for reform on the basis of the Qurʾan and the sunna of the Prophet, he aspired in fact to the overthrow of the Umayyad caliphate. Soon he adopted for his dress and his flags the black color associated with the messianic restorer of Islam and asked for a consultative council *(shūrā)* to choose the most acceptable candidate for the caliphate. His propaganda indeed intimated that he would be the one "to destroy the walls of Damascus" and to put an end to the Umayyad regime though he had to admit that his companions would not pledge allegiance to him on that basis.[3]

His alliance with the infidel enemies of the Muslims as well as his

3. Al-Ṭabarī, *Taʾrīkh,* II, p. 1919.

adoption of extreme theological and political positions cost al-Ḥārith the backing of the moderate Murjiʾa in Khurasan including some of those who had been involved with Abu l-Ṣaydāʾ in encouraging the resistance of the Soghdian converts to the payment of *jizya*. The leading figure among the Murjiʾa in Iraq at this time, Abū Ḥanīfa, certainly also did not view the radical revolutionary movement with favor. Abū Ḥanīfa was a strong protagonist of reform under the Qurʾanic maxim of "ordering what is proper and forbidding the reprehensible," but he was generally opposed to armed revolt. He is also known to have spoken out against some of the extreme theological views of Jahm b. Ṣafwān. Yet his break with the radicals was evidently not complete. In 126/744 al-Ḥārith b. Surayj was seeking a pardon from the reform-minded caliph Yazīd III. His two emissaries passed through Kufa where they requested and received a letter of introduction from Abū Ḥanīfa to the caliphal court in Damascus.

The moderate Murjiʾa of the tendency of Abū Ḥanīfa became the heirs of the popular allegiance initially enjoyed by al-Ḥārith b. Surayj. The doctrinal and legal school of Abū Ḥanīfa spread rapidly in the very areas where al-Ḥārith had recruited his early following, in Lower Ṭukhāristān. Balkh in particular became an early bastion of eastern Ḥanafism. In Kufa it was even dubbed Murjiʾābād, Murjiʾa-town, presumably by the adversaries of Abū Ḥanīfa. The reason for this was, according to the city historian of Balkh Ṣafī al-Dīn al-Wāʿiẓ al-Balkhī, that Abū Ḥanīfa was called a Murjiʾite and all the people of Balkh were adherents of his doctrine. While the students from other parts of Khurasan travelling to Iraq in the quest of learning joined different scholars there, those from Balkh invariably preferred Abū Ḥanīfa as their teacher.

The first Ḥanafite *qāḍī* in Balkh was appointed in 142/759–760, still in the lifetime of the founder of the school. He was ʿUmar b. Maymūn al-Rammāḥ, a student and close companion of Abū Ḥanīfa, who retained his office for more than twenty years. His successor, Abū Muḥammad al-Aʿmash, was appointed by the locally much-detested ʿAbbasid governor of Khurasan, ʿAlī b. ʿĪsā b. Māhān. Al-Aʿmash persecuted some popular Ḥanafite scholars and was later ignominiously chased out of the town by the people. He was succeeded by Abū Muṭīʿ al-Ḥakam b. ʿAbd Allāh al-Balkhī, another pupil of Abū Ḥanīfa and leading propagator of his Murjiʾite theological teaching in the east. Abū Muṭīʿ is the author of the so-called *al-Fiqh al-absaṭ* in which he set forth Abū Ḥanīfa's answers to theological questions. He is also the transmitter of the *Kitāb al-ʿĀlim wa l-mutaʿallim* of Abū Muqātil al-

Samarqandī, a treatise explicitly espousing the doctrine of *irjāʾ* and formulated by the author on behalf of his teacher Abū Ḥanīfa. Together with Abū Ḥanīfa's *Risāla ilā ʿUthmān al-Battī,* these two texts provided the foundation of all later Murjiʾite theology of eastern Ḥanafism.

The practical relevance of Abū Ḥanīfa's doctrine of *irjāʾ* to the situation of the eastern converts to Islam is readily apparent in its formulation in these works. In *al-Fiqh al-absaṭ* Abū Muṭīʿ al-Balkhī reports that he asked Abū Ḥanīfa about the status of a Muslim in the territory of polytheism *(arḍ al-shirk)* who assents to Islam as a whole but has no knowledge of the Qurʾan or any of the religious duties of Islam. Abū Ḥanīfa answered that such a man would be a believer (*muʾmin*).[4] The mention of the territory of polytheism illustrates the circumstances under which ignorance of the Qurʾan and the religious duties of the Muslim could be excusable for a convert. Neither Abū Ḥanīfa nor the Murjiʾite theologians in general were moral laxists prepared to condone ignorance or disregard of the religious law as they were sometimes accused by their opponents. They held, no doubt, that every effort must be made to teach the converts the duties of Islam. Their concern was basically with the legal status of the converts and their essential equality in the name of justice. Abū Ḥanīfa backed up his position through reference to the situation at the beginning of the prophetic mission of Muḥammad when he merely summoned men to testify to the unity of God and to assent to whatever he would reveal from God. Anyone accepting this condition was called a believer even though he could not fulfill any of the religious duties which were revealed only later.[5] Similarly the convert who "assents to Islam as a whole" becomes a true believer even though he may not yet know and practice any of the duties of Islam. Abū Ḥanīfa went to extremes in maintaining that there are no ranks or degrees of faith among the Muslims. In *al-Fiqh al-absaṭ* and the *Kitāb al-ʿĀlim wa l-mutaʿallim* he is quoted as affirming that the faith of every Muslim is identical with that of the prophets and the angels.[6]

Murjiʾite Ḥanafism continued to expand in eastern Iran after the time of Abū Muṭīʿ al-Balkhī. By the third/ninth century Ṭukhāristān and Transoxania became overwhelmingly Ḥanafite. The number of Arab settlers in these provinces had been relatively small and it was

4. In other Transoxanian Ḥanafite texts *arḍ al-shirk* is replaced by *arḍ al-Turk,* territory of the Turks. "The Spread of Māturīdism and the Turks," p. 122.
5. "Early Sunnī Doctrine concerning Faith," p. 236.
6. Schacht, p. 107; "Early Sunnī Doctrine concerning Faith," pp. 242–243.

mainly, though not exclusively, the non-Arab converts who were attracted to the egalitarian creed of the school. Ḥanafism here took on a distinctly populist character. It prided itself to be the Islam of "the great mass," *al-sawād al-aʿẓam,* as implied by the name of a popular Transoxanian Ḥanafite creed. Transoxanian Ḥanafites indeed came to consider their school as exclusively constituting the *ahl al-sunna wa l-jamāʿa.*[7]

The eastern Murjiʾa, though ready to resist the Umayyad administrative practice, did not join the ʿAbbasid revolutionary movement and came, according to the testimony of the city history of Balkh, equally in conflict with the early ʿAbbasid administration.[8] After Abū Muslim emerged in public as the leader of the anti-Umayyad revolution and occupied Marw, he sent Abū Dāwūd Khālid b. Ibrāhīm al-Bakrī in 130/747–748 to subdue Ṭukhāristān. The latter soon expelled the Umayyad governor from Balkh. As soon as he was recalled to Marw, all the Arabs and *mawālī* in Ṭukhāristān united, and Abū Dāwūd's successor in Balkh made common cause with them to fight Abū Muslim. The command was given to Muqātil b. Ḥayyān al-Nabaṭī, the leader of the *mawālī.* Black flags were used by some of the allies, and they may well have been, as suggested by Wellhausen,[9] those of al-Ḥārith b. Surayj. In Balkh the popular opposition to Abū Muslim's forces was led by the religious leaders, Mutawakkil b. Ḥumrān, Muqātil b. Sulaymān, and Abū Ḥanīfa's disciple Ibn al-Rammāḥ. When Abū Dāwūd al-Bakrī defeated the allies and reoccupied Balkh, they were forced to go into hiding until he granted them a pardon.

There is also some evidence of a clash between Abū Muslim and the moderate Murjiʾa in Marw. In 131/748–749 two prominent Murjiʾites, one of them a companion of Abū Ḥanīfa, were executed there because of their public censure of his conduct. No further details about the circumstances are available. It is evident, however, that the Murjiʾa were more concerned with their demands for reform than with the overthrow of the Umayyad caliphate. As already noted, they had also failed to back the ambitions of al-Ḥārith b. Surayj in this regard.

In Balkh, the center of the eastern Murjiʾa, hostility to the ʿAbbasid government remained strong. Only a few representative examples from the city history of Balkh may be quoted here. After pardoning the religious leaders of the town, Abū Dāwūd appointed Mutawakkil

7. "The Spread of Māturīdism and the Turks," pp. 117, 134–135.
8. "The Early Murjiʾa," p. 38, n. 25.
9. J. Wellhausen, *Das arabische Reich und sein Sturz,* p. 334.

b. Ḥumrān *qāḍī.* The latter stipulated that he would not name Abū Dāwūd as the governor on the pulpit and would not accept the testimony of representatives of the government in court. He rejected a prohibition of the caliph to render judgment concerning caliphal property and returned the official letter with an appropriate Qurʾanic quotation. When he ran into trouble with the governor and was put to death, the people closed their shops for a long time as a sign of mourning. Salm b. Sālim al-Balkhī is described by Ibn Saᶜd[10] as a Murjiʾite weak in *ḥadīth*[11] but stern in "ordering what is proper and forbidding the reprehensible." He had a position of religious leadership in Khurasan. The city history of Balkh describes him as professing to have no doubt that it was illicit to look the unjust ruler or his helpers in the face. The only question was whether speaking to them was permissible or not. The governor ᶜAlī b. ᶜĪsā b. Māhān complained to the caliph that Salm disregarded the caliph's signature and refused the testimony of government officials. As a result, Salm was arrested while visiting Baghdad and was kept in prison until the death of the caliph Hārūn al-Rashīd.

Reformist *irjāʾ* came into conflict during the Umayyad age with administrative practice and with conservative and traditionalist Islam. Traditionalist Islam, no doubt, commanded the allegiance of the great majority of the Arab settlers and of the early Iranian converts most closely associated with them. The sources, however, provide little information on traditionalist Islam and its representatives in Iran during that period. Ibn Saᶜd offers an impressive list of traditionists active in Khurasan and a much smaller one for western Iran,[12] obviously reflecting the preponderance of early Arab settlement in the east. Most of these traditionists flourished in the early ᶜAbbasid age. The first Khurasanian traditionist who gained wide fame was ᶜAbd Allāh b. Mubārak of Marw (d. 181/797), son of a Turkish father and a Khurasanian mother.[13] In Iran no early center of Islamic traditionist learning arose comparable to Medina, Mekka, Kufa, Basra, Damascus, or Ḥimṣ. These early centers of Islamic scholarship developed rival schools with sometimes widely divergent religious and legal views. Early traditionalist Islam was thus not doctrinally uniform although it implied a general religious conservatism. While some of the ten-

10. Ibn Saᶜd, *K. al-Ṭabaqāt al-kabīr,* VII/2, p. 106.
11. According to the city history of Balkh he transmitted from Abū Ḥanīfa. ᶜAbd Allāh b. ᶜUmar Wāᶜiẓ-i Balkhī, *Faḍāʾil Balkh,* ed. ᶜAbd al-Ḥayy Ḥabībī, p. 160.
12. Ibn Saᶜd, VII/2, pp. 101–109 (Khurasan), 109–111 (Ray, Hamadan, Qom).
13. Al-Khaṭīb al-Baghdādī, *Taʾrīkh Baghdād,* X, p. 153.

dencies of the early traditionist schools and currents in the major towns of the central Islamic territories can clearly be defined, very little is known about the currents and tendencies of traditionalism in early Islamic Iran. The strongest was presumably the influence of Basra from where most of the Arab settlers and early traditionists came. Certainly there predominated a loyalist Islam, attached to the historical caliphate, if not specifically to the House of the Umayyads. Khārijite and Shiʿite currents were present in some regions but were generally marginal.

While Khurasan did not produce a distinctive early school of traditionalism, Khurasanians, or Khurasanian emigrants, were to found and sustain the most important traditionalist school in Sunnite Islam at the peak of the ʿAbbasid caliphate. Ḥanbalism, the school of Aḥmad b. Ḥanbal, is usually viewed as a product of Baghdad and the Arab world—and naturally so, since its founder was an Arab active throughout his life in Baghdad and where Ḥanbalism later commanded its broadest popular support. Little attention has been paid to the fact that Ibn Ḥanbal's family was of Khurasanian origin and that most of his backing came from the quarters of Baghdad settled by Khurasanians. Aḥmad b. Ḥanbal's grandfather, Ḥanbal b. Hilāl, belonged to a Basran Arab family which settled in Marw and was won over to the ʿAbbasid revolutionary movement. Presumably in reward for his services, he was appointed ʿAbbasid governor of Sarakhs. Aḥmad's father Muḥammad, too, was a commander (*qāʾid*) in the ʿAbbasid army. He moved to Baghdad where Aḥmad was born, a few months after the family's arrival, in the year 164/780.[14] It seems thus appropriate to raise the question of the significance of this Khurasanian aspect in the genesis of Ḥanbalism.

Ḥanbalism can be viewed as an attempt to transcend the regional traditionalist schools and currents and to create a uniform religious and legal doctrine based on the most valid traditions contained in each of them. For this purpose the new discipline of *ḥadīth* criticism was developed. The need to choose between equally well attested traditions also encouraged a hierarchical ranking of religious excellence and authority. The environment of the newly founded capital was obviously well suited for this effort to overcome the regional divisions of the early traditionalist schools. And the Khurasanians settling in Baghdad, having no strong local tradition of their own to defend, could more readily than others take up the task.

14. *Taʾrīkh Baghdād,* IV, p. 415. Ḥanbal b. Hilāl was punished in Bukhara by the Umayyad governor for subverting the army.

The Khurasanian emigrants in Baghdad were, on the other hand, predominantly Arab. They came initially as members of the Khurasanian army and their families. Aḥmad b. Ḥanbal and his family were representative of them. He was, as the sources stress, of purely Arab extraction. Arab Khurasanians were no doubt generally more inclined to settle permanently in Baghdad than Iranians. There were, of course, also families of Iranians who came to Baghdad in the service of the ʿAbbasids, some of them in high positions. But they were certainly a minority and many of them are known to have adhered to heterodoxy and Shiʿism.

Arab sentiments are reflected in one of Ibn Ḥanbal's creeds where he mentions the *shuʿūbiyya* among the condemnable religious sects describing them as misguided heretics who say: "The Arabs and the *mawālī* are in our view equal! They do not recognize any right (of priority) for them, nor do they acknowledge any excellence in them. They do not love them, but rather they hate the Arabs and conceal rancor, envy, and loathing of them in their hearts."[15]

It would be unfair to accuse Ibn Ḥanbal of anti-Persian prejudice and of advocating superior rights for the Arabs in general. Merit and excellence were based for him exclusively in Islam. Yet he evidently wished the superior merit of the Arab Muslims at the rise of Islam, which was at the same time its ideal, exemplary age, to be permanently recognized. The hierarchy of excellence in Islam was irreversibly weighted in favor of the Arabs.

The vigorous condemnation of *irjāʾ* by Ḥanbalism may also in part be related to the egalitarian definition of faith by the Murjiʾa. Abū Ḥanīfa and the Murjiʾa in general did not deny, of course, disparity of merit and religious excellence on the basis of worship and acts. But their rejection of any difference of rank in faith, the most essential quality of Islam, and their claim that the faith of any late convert who ignored the Qurʾan and all religious duties of Islam was equal to that of the Prophet must have seemed contrary to all good sense to men so deeply concerned with upholding and restoring the traditional hierarchy of excellence in Islam.

As against the heterodoxy and Shiʿism of so many prominent servants of the ʿAbbasid regime, Ḥanbalism embodied strictest Sunnism. It must seem most striking that a religious movement arising among the descendants of the revolutionaries who had brought the ʿAbbasids to power and who continued to back their caliphate most solidly re-

15. Ibn Abī Yaʿlā, *Ṭabaqāt al-Ḥanābila,* I, p. 34.

pudiated the religious motives of that revolution. It confirms the view that the Shiʿite core of the ʿAbbasid movement, while it attracted wide popular Iranian allegiance, remained small and that the great majority of the Khurasanian army joined it late and without much sympathy for its Shiʿite principles. Political considerations soon led the ʿAbbasid caliphs to distance themselves more and more from the small ʿAbbasid Shīʿa that remained loyal after the schism of the supporters of Abū Muslim. Under Hārūn al-Rashīd it was completely suppressed and disintegrated. The Ḥanbalites of Baghdad became the staunchest supporters of the ʿAbbasids. They backed them not as Shiʿite imams of the Family of the Prophet, but as heirs of the historical caliphate. Rehabilitation of the Umayyads was a major concern of Ḥanbalite ideology.

Ibn Ḥanbal's strict anti-Shiʿism was also reflected in his adoption of the early Medinese view of the caliphate, which was upheld also by many Syrian traditionists. This was based on a *ḥadīth* ascribed to ʿAbd Allāh b. ʿUmar according to which the Companions in the time of Muḥammad had been agreed that the most excellent Muslims after the Prophet were Abū Bakr, ʿUmar, and ʿUthmān. It was understood to mean that only these three were the legitimate successors of the Prophet and Rightly-guided Caliphs and that after them the caliphate was based merely on power.[16] This view excluding ʿAlī from the legitimate caliphate was in the time of Ibn Ḥanbal already a minority opinion in Sunnism, especially in Iraq. Ibn Ḥanbal later in his life changed his position to include ʿAlī among the Rightly-guided Caliphs. He continued to insist, however, that the four caliphs must be ranked in excellence in accordance with their sequence. ʿUthmān must thus be preferred to ʿAlī. He expressly rejected a mere preference of Abū Bakr and ʿUmar over the two later caliphs, although he refrained from condemning those failing to mention the superiority of ʿUthmān as heretics remarking: "What would we do with the Kufans?" The preference of only the first two caliphs was the doctrine of the prominent Kufan traditionist Sufyān al-Thawrī who was otherwise greatly admired by Ibn Ḥanbal for his outspoken condemnation of the doctrine of the creation of the Qurʾan and of the Murjiʾa.[17]

While Ḥanbalism viewed the reign of the first three or four caliphs as the only true caliphate based on inherent legitimacy of merit, it equally made loyalty to the later historical caliphate, based on power,

16. *Der Imam al-Qāsim,* pp. 225–226.
17. "The Origins of the Controversy Concerning the Creation of the Koran," p. 519.

a fundamental religious duty. Ḥanbalite theory of the caliphate went further than Sunnite doctrine in general in affirming the validity of the caliphate by usurpation (*ghalaba*). Yet the caliph must belong to the Quraysh until the end of time. It was the duty of every Muslim to obey and assist him and his representatives, whether he was righteous or evil, just or oppressive. A passage from one of Ibn Ḥanbal's creeds may again be quoted: "The caliphate belongs to Quraysh as long as there remain even two people. No one of the people has the right to dispute their title to it and to revolt against them. We do not affirm it for anyone but them until the day of the Resurrection. The *jihād* is a permanent obligation together with the imams, whether they are righteous or sinners; neither oppression of the oppressors nor justice of the just can cancel it. The congregational Friday prayer, the feasts, and the pilgrimage with the rulers are obligatory, even if they are not virtuous, just, and pious. Payment of the alms tax, the land tax, the tithes (is a duty), and surrender of war booty to the commanders, whether they be just or unjust. Submission to the one whom God has put in charge of your command (is obligatory); do not withdraw your hand from obedience to him and do not come forward against him with your sword, (but be patient) until God may give you relief and an escape. Do not revolt against the ruler, but hear and obey, and do not break an oath of allegiance. Whoever does that is an innovator who opposes, and abandons, the Community (*jamāʿa*). If the ruler commands you to do an act of disobedience towards God do not obey him at all; but you do not have the right to sedition against him. Do not prevent him from his right."[18]

This affirmation of unquestioning backing of the established caliphate clearly reflects the situation and the spirit of the Khurasanian loyalists in the Umayyad age in their permanent *jihād* against the infidels beyond the borders of Islam. It was the spirit of that heroic age which their descendants living in Baghdad longed to revive, although their struggle now was more against heresy inside the world of Islam than against the infidels outside its territories. The ʿAbbasid revolution, in which their ancestors had become embroiled, had been an illegitimate rebellion against the established caliphate in violation of the true principles of Islam. But the ʿAbbasid caliphate, though first based on usurpation, was now established fact. It was entitled to unquestioning loyalty, except in disobedience to the orders of God.

18. Ibn Abī Yaʿlā, I, pp. 26–27.

The Two Factions of Sunnism: Ḥanafism and Shāfiᶜism

From the Buwayhid age on Sunnite Muslims in Iran mostly belonged to either of two legal schools, founded by Abū Ḥanīfa and al-Shāfiᶜī. In view of their overwhelming preponderance and the common rivalry between them, they were often referred to simply as the "two factions (*farīqān*)." The circumstances of the early spread of the Ḥanafite school in eastern Iran, still in the first half of the second/eighth century, have already been discussed. Shāfiᶜism expanded in Iran on a substantial scale only in the later third/ninth century.[1] In the teaching career of the founder of the school two phases are usually distinguished. The legal doctrine taught by him during his stay in Baghdad from 194–198/810–814 is known as "the old (*al-qadīm*)," while that of his final activity in Egypt 198–204/814–820 is known as "the new (*al-jadīd*)." The old doctrine soon became extinct, although one of al-Shāfiᶜī's students of the Baghdad period, Abū Thawr al-Kalbī, founded on its basis his own legal school which subsequently spread in Armenia and Adharbayjan. Al-Shāfiᶜī's new doctrine was first systematized by his Egyptian pupils, al-Muzanī, author of the famous *Mukhtaṣar,* Ḥarmala, al-Buwayṭī, Yūnus b. ᶜAbd al-Aᶜlā, and al-Rabīᶜ b. Sulaymān, who compiled and transmitted their master's works under the title *Kitāb al-Umm.* Only in the following generation was it carried east. In Baghdad its first teachers were ᶜUthmān b. Saᶜīd al-Anmāṭī and, more importantly, Abu l-ᶜAbbās b. Surayj (d. 306/918–919), who was also *qāḍī* of Shiraz for some time. In the same period it was introduced in Nishapur by Muḥammad b. Naṣr al-Marwazī and Muḥammad b. Isḥāq b. Khuzayma (d. 311/923). The former moved in 275/888–889 on to Samarqand, where he enjoyed the patronage of the Sāmānid Ismāᶜīl b. Aḥmad, and taught there until his death in 294/906–907. While Nishapur, however, came to shelter a large and vigorous Shāfiᶜite community, the Shāfiᶜite presence in Samarqand remained insignificant in the face of the strong Ḥanafite preponderance. Still further northeast, Shāsh (Tashkent) with Īlāq and Ṭarāz, became a predominantly Shāfiᶜite enclave, partly through the teaching activity of the renowned Shāfiᶜite scholar Abū Bakr Muḥammad b. ᶜAlī al-Qaffāl (d. 365/976). In western and central Iran Shāfiᶜism was

1. For the following see in general H. Halm, *Die Ausbreitung der šāfiᶜitischen Rechtsschule,* pp. 15–154.

introduced in the major towns like Isfahan, Shiraz, Ray, and Gorgan from the middle of the third/ninth century and soon established sizable communities. By the beginning of the fifth/eleventh century it had clearly gained the edge over Ḥanafism in some towns and regions of western Iran and held the balance against it in Iran as a whole. Only the most eastern regions, Transoxania, Ṭukhāristān, Ghazna and the Turkish and Indian territories beyond, remained overwhelmingly Ḥanafite with only small Shāfiʿite minorities.

The Shāfiʿite legal school initially spread in Iran mainly in traditionist circles. In the early time the Shāfiʿites indeed often identified themselves, and were identified, as *ahl ḥadīth* or as the jurists, *fuqahāʾ*, of the *ahl al-ḥadīth.* Some of the leading early protagonists of Shāfiʿism, like Ibn Khuzayma in Nishapur and Abū Bakr al-Ismāʿīlī (d. 371/981) in Gorgan, were equally or more active as traditionists. Al-Shāfiʿī himself had, of course, been at the forefront of the struggle to give *ḥadīth,* and in particular the *ḥadīth* of the Prophet, overriding authority in the law and had severely criticized the schools of Abū Ḥanīfa and Mālik for what he saw as their disregard of tradition. It was thus natural that the traditionalists in Iran in their opposition to Ḥanafism, identified by them as the school of speculative opinion (*raʾy*), were attracted to the school of al-Shāfiʿī. As the spread of Shāfiʿism gained momentum it also largely absorbed the minor communities of other legal schools inclining to traditionalism. Thus it replaced the school of Sufyān al-Thawrī, the traditionalist rival of Abū Ḥanīfa in Kufa, which had gained some early support in Isfahan, Dīnawar and Hamadan. Likewise it supplanted the Ẓāhiriyya in Shiraz, the school of Mālik in Ahvaz, and Ḥanbalism in Gorgan, Ray, and Qazvin.[2] In part perhaps because it was considered primarily a theological rather than a legal school and because of its strong political engagement, Ḥanbalism never attracted much popular following in Iran. Only the people of western Gilan who were converted to Islam by a Ḥanbalite from Amol, Abū Jaʿfar al-Thūmī, in the latter part of the third/ninth century,[3] remained solidly Ḥanbalite until the Mongol age.

Shāfiʿism, unlike Ḥanafism and Ḥanbalism, was essentially a legal school with no strong ties to any theological doctrine or school. Although a credal *waṣiyya* was transmitted from al-Shāfiʿī,[4] it did not become subject to theological elaboration and systematization among

2. Al-Maqdisī, *Aḥsan al-taqāsīm fī maʿrifat al-aqālīm,* pp. 365, 395, 415, 439.
3. See "Abū Isḥāq al-Ṣābī on the Alids of Ṭabaristān and Gīlān," pp. 29–30.
4. F. Kern, "Ein dogmatisches Vermächtnis des Imām aš-Šāfiʿī," in *MSOS* XIII, pp. 141–145.

the Shāfiʿites as did the *Fiqh al-akhbar* attributed to Abū Ḥanīfa among the Ḥanafites. The early Shāfiʿites, in Iran and elsewhere, were certainly not united in their religious views. Most of them evidently inclined to traditionalism in theology as in law and were opposed to the speculative reasoning of *kalām*. Traditionalism, however, did not entail a uniform position on many theological questions, and it would be a mistake to assume that most Shāfiʿites were in fact Ḥanbalites in theology. There were also more rationalist currents in early Shāfiʿism. Ibn Surayj is said to have frequented Abu l-Ḥusayn al-Khayyāṭ, chief of the Muʿtazila of Baghdad, and to have adopted some of his teaching.[5] Abū Bakr al-Qaffāl was accused of being a Muʿtazilī, probably wrongly, but he is known to have taken more rationalist positions in his legal methodology than were approved in later mainstream Shāfiʿism.[6]

A development of far-reaching consequences was the adoption of Ashʿarī theology by the Shāfiʿites in Nishapur in the early fifth/eleventh century. Two famous Ashʿarī *kalām* scholars, Abū Bakr b. Fūrak (d. 406/1015) and Abū Isḥāq al-Isfarāyīnī (d. 418/1027), having studied in Baghdad, came to teach in the metropolis of Khurasan at this time. The cause of Ashʿarism was taken up by some of the leading Shāfiʿite families of Nishapur and it was henceforth firmly established in the town which had become the major center of Shāfiʿite learning in the east. Ashʿarism then spread quickly among the other Shāfiʿite communities in Iran, partly from Nishapur, and partly straight from Iraq. During the Saljūq age it became the predominant theology of the Shāfiʿites throughout the Islamic world, although there always remained some traditionalist opposition, influenced by Ḥanbalism, in the Shāfiʿite school.[7] The strength of Ashʿarism among the Shāfiʿites must not be measured, of course, by the relatively small number of those who actually practiced or formally studied Ashʿarī *kalām*. Rather it is reflected by the acceptance of Ashʿarī creeds and Ashʿarī legal methodology by the great majority of the Shāfiʿites.

Ashʿarism in Nishapur, moreover, moved away from the Ḥanbalite dogmatic positions which al-Ashʿarī himself had set out to defend with the rational methods of *kalām* and to which al-Bāqillānī, the prominent Ashʿarī contemporary of Ibn Fūrak and Abū Isḥāq al-Isfarāyīnī in Baghdad, mostly continued to adhere. Ibn Fūrak endeavored to interpret the anthropomorphic expressions in *ḥadīth* metaphorically

5. Ibn al-Murtaḍā, *Ṭabaqāt al-Muʿtazila,* p. 129.
6. Halm, p. 113.
7. "The Spread of Māturīdism and the Turks," pp. 109–110.

while avoiding the more radical interpretations of the Muʿtazila.[8] Abū Isḥāq al-Isfarāyīnī was evidently even more deeply influenced by Muʿtazilī views.[9] It was eastern Ashʿarism developing in Nishapur which often saw itself as a golden mean between the extremes of *tashbīh* and *jabr,* anthropomorphism and determinism, on the one hand, and Muʿtazilism, on the other.

Ḥanafism in Iran and Iraq was also lacking unity in its theological doctrine. There was the usual disagreement between those inclined to traditionalism and those favorably disposed to *kalām.* Not all Ḥanafites, moreover, tried to follow the theological teaching attributed to Abū Ḥanīfa. In particular Muʿtazilism made big inroads among the Ḥanafite communities in Iraq and western Iran. In its original home, Basra, the theological school of the Muʿtazila appears gradually to have become associated with adherence to Ḥanafism in law and ritual. Muʿtazilism spread from Basra east to Khuzistan and Fars and evidently gained a broad popular following in towns like Ahvaz, Rāmhormoz, Tustar, ʿAskar Mukram, Sīrāf, and Ṣaymara.[10] Most of the Muʿtazilīs there presumably belonged to the Ḥanafite community. In Baghdad the relationship between Muʿtazilī theologians like Abū ʿAbd Allāh al-Baṣrī (d. 369/981) and the Ḥanafite legal school was close, and a number of prominent Ḥanafite legal scholars like Abu l-Ḥasan al-Karkhī (d. 340/951), Abū Bakr al-Rāzī (d. 370/981), and Abū ʿAbd Allāh al-Ṣaymarī (d. 436/1045) were Muʿtazilīs.[11]

In Ray, where there was a strong community of Ḥanafites from an early date, they adhered during the third/ninth and the first half of the fourth/tenth centuries to the theological school of al-Ḥusayn al-Najjār (fl. 200/815). The school had also a substantial following in the environs of Ray, in Qazvin and Gorgan.[12] The Najjāriyya were a specifically Ḥanafite school of *kalām.* They were Murjiʾite in their definition of faith, strictly predestinarian, but close to the Muʿtazila in their anti-anthropomorphist doctrine concerning the attributes of God. In view of this combination of basic theological views, they were often counted among the Jahmiyya, though there is no evidence that they looked to Jahm b. Ṣafwān as one of their teachers.[13] In the Bu-

8. M. Watt, "Ibn Fūrak," in *E.I.*, 2nd ed.
9. "Al-Isfarāyīnī," in *E.I.*, 2nd ed.
10. Abu l-Qāsim al-Balkhī in ʿAbd al-Jabbār, *Faḍl al-iʿtizāl,* ed. F. Sayyid, pp. 111ff.; al-Maqdisī, pp. 410, 413, 415.
11. "The Spread of Māturīdism and the Turks," p. 112.
12. "The Spread of Māturīdism and the Turks," p. 113.
13. See J. van Ess, "Ḍirār b. ʿAmr und die Cahmiyya," in *Der Islam* XLIV, pp. 56–63.

wayhid age, however, Ray also became a center of Muᶜtazilism. This was due in particular to the efforts of the Buwayhid vizier al-Ṣāḥib b. ᶜAbbād who appointed the leading Muᶜtazilī scholar of the time, ᶜAbd al-Jabbār al-Hamadhānī (d. 415/1024–1025), *qāḍī l-quḍāt* in Ray and, according to al-Maqdisī,[14] sent Muᶜtazilī missionaries to the Ḥanafite communities in the region. Although Qāḍī ᶜAbd al-Jabbār personally was a Shāfiᶜite, his impact as a teacher was evidently strongest among the Ḥanafites and the Shiᶜites, Imāmīs and Zaydīs, who also enjoyed the favor of al-Ṣāḥib b. ᶜAbbād. The conquest of Ray by Maḥmūd of Ghazna in 420/1029 and his burning of Muᶜtazilī and other heretical books there was a severe blow to the Muᶜtazila, but did not permanently break their influence. One of the most prominent and widely respected Ḥanafite scholars in Ray in the early Saljūq age, Ismāᶜīl b. ᶜAlī al-Sammān, actively propagated Muᶜtazilī *kalām*. The Najjāriyya maintained their position in the town though they apparently no longer produced any theologians of rank. In the middle of the sixth/twelfth century they were still in control of the old congregational mosque, while the other Ḥanafites assembled in a newer mosque built by the Saljūq sultan Ṭughril-beg.

In eastern Iran and Transoxania the theological tradition building on the creeds and doctrinal elaborations transmitted by Abū Muṭīᶜ al-Balkhī from Abū Ḥanīfa remained alive. Ḥanafism gained the status of an official religion under the Sāmānid dynasty. The Sāmānid Ismāᶜīl b. Aḥmad (279–295/892–907) is reported to have assembled the scholars of Samarqand, Bukhara and other towns in Transoxania and ordered them to set forth the Sunnite dogma in the face of the spread of heresy. They commissioned Abu l-Qāsim al-Ḥakīm al-Samarqandī (d. 342/953), a Ḥanafite scholar with Sufi leanings and later *qāḍi* of Samarqand, to compose a statement of the orthodox creed. After its completion it was formally approved by the scholars and the ruler. This popular creed known under the name of *al-Sawād al-aᶜẓam* became the official catechism under the Sāmānids and was in the later Sāmānid age also translated into Persian.[15]

A contemporary of Abu l-Qāsim al-Ḥakīm also living in Samarqand, Abū Manṣūr al-Māturīdī (d. 332/944), became the founder of a doctrinal school which in more modern times has been recognized as the second orthodox Sunnite school of *kalām* besides Ashᶜarism.[16] Like al-Ashᶜarī, al-Maturīdī was mainly concerned with meeting the challenge

14. Al-Maqdisī, p. 395.
15. See "Abu l-Qāsem Esḥāq Samarqandī," in *E.Ir.*
16. See "al-Māturīdī," in *E.I.*, 2nd ed.

of Muʿtazilī *kalām*. Yet while al-Ashʿarī based his *kalām* on Ḥanbalite traditionalist dogma, al-Māturīdī built upon the eastern Ḥanafite tradition. His theology was in substance less extreme in its antagonism against the Muʿtazila, but also less influenced by their technical concepts than that of al-Ashʿarī who had himself at first been a Muʿtazilī theologian. In contrast to the fate of al-Ashʿarī, who was repudiated by the faction whose creed he strove to defend rationally, i.e., the Ḥanbalites, al-Māturīdī remained firmly within the Ḥanafite community of Samarqand and did not arouse any opposition among his colleagues there except on some minor questions. Some of the points later considered characteristic of Māturīdism are known to have been upheld in Samarqand already two generations before al-Māturīdī. His teaching thus was generally referred to as the doctrine of the scholars of Samarqand, if it was not simply identified as that of Abū Ḥanīfa, and only many centuries later the name Māturīdiyya became common for the school. In the fourth/tenth century there were still a few points of disagreement in theological matters between the scholars of Samarqand and those of Bukhara, who tended to be more anti-rationalist and closer to the Ashʿarite positions. These were commonly bridged over with compromise solutions by the later representatives of Māturīdism as it became the universally accepted theology of eastern Ḥanafism.

While Ḥanafism came under increasing pressure from the west by the rapid expansion of Shāfiʿism in much of Iran during the third/ninth and fourth/tenth centuries, it was greatly reinforced in the east by the conversion of the Turks throughout Central Asia as far as Balāsāghūn, Kāshghar and Khotan to Islam. Few details are known about the process of the conversion of the Turks. It has often been suggested that Sufi preachers and dervishes were chiefly responsible for the conversion and that Sufism of an unorthodox nature and Shiʿism were widespread among the early Turkish converts. There is, however, abundant evidence that the overwhelming majority of the Turks converted in Central Asia became staunch Ḥanafites. If Sufi preachers played a role in their conversion they evidently represented popular eastern Ḥanafism. It may be noted here that Abū Ḥanīfa's statement about the status of a Muslim who assents to Islam as a whole without any knowledge of the Qurʾan and the religious duties of Islam "in the territory of Polytheism *(fī arḍ al-shirk)*" appears in later Māturīdī quotations with a slight graphical change as referring to "the territory of the Turks." Evidently it had acquired specific significance to the situation of the Turkish nomads who might be eager to confess their adherence to Islam without being able or willing to learn the details of its ritual and law.

With the Saljūq expansion in the fifth/eleventh century, Turks spread all over Iran and further west as a conquering ruling class.[17] Historians have sometimes viewed the Saljūq age as a time of growing Sunnite solidarity in the face of the Ismāʿīlī danger. Saljūq military superiority indeed brought about a restoration of Sunnite ascendancy culminating in the overthrow of the Fatimid caliphate which at the time of Ṭughril-beg's invasion of Iraq had for a moment threatened the ʿAbbasid capital Baghdad itself. Yet the main effect of the Saljūq expansion on the religious scene, in particular in Iran, was anything but Sunnite solidarity. The attempt of the Saljūqs to establish Ḥanafism everywhere as the official religion, giving preference to Ḥanafites in all religious and government appointments and patronage, led to a major clash between the Ḥanafite and the Shāfiʿite communities in the major Iranian cities resulting in recurrent factional war and extensive destruction in the later Saljūq and post-Saljūq age. Vigorous factional rivalry between the Ḥanafites and Shāfiʿites had indeed been common in Persian towns already in the fourth/tenth century as observed by the traveler and geographer al-Maqdisī. There was, however, a general balance of power, traditional rights and privileges which restrained potential violence. This balance was now disturbed by the overt partisanship of the Saljūq rulers and the crude Ḥanafite fanaticism and anti-Shāfiʿite bias of many of the Turks settling in the garrison towns in Iran. The Shāfiʿite reaction was equally powerful.

Already the founder of the Saljūq empire in Iran and Iraq, Ṭughril-beg, saw to it that the Ḥanafite ritual prevailed in the congregational Mosques in his residential towns and appointed only Ḥanafite *qāḍī*s there. In Nishapur he used the occasion of a quarrel between Ḥanafites and Shāfiʿites about the orthodoxy of al-Ashʿarī to dismiss the Shāfiʿite *khaṭīb* of the mosque, Abū ʿUthmān al-Ṣābūnī, and appointed a succession of Ḥanafites. Thus the ritual, which traditionally had been Shāfiʿite, was changed to the Ḥanafite. The position of *qāḍī,* which traditionally had already been held by Ḥanafites, was left in the hands of the Ḥanafite Ṣāʿidī family. Ṭughril-beg also built and endowed a *madrasa,* known as the Sulṭāniyya, for the benefit of the Ḥanafites in Nishapur.[18]

In Ray, Ṭughril-beg strengthened the Ḥanafites by building a sec-

17. For the following see in general "The Spread of Māturīdism and the Turks," pp. 126ff.

18. R. W. Bulliet, *The Patricians of Nishapur,* p. 252.

ond congregational mosque for them. He brought two members of the Ṣāʿidī family of Nishapur, Abu l-Ḥasan Ismāʿīl b. Ṣāʿid and Abū Saʿd Yaḥyā b. Muḥammad, to Ray as his chief *qāḍīs*. In Isfahan he appointed the Ḥanafite ʿAlī b. ʿUbayd Allāh al-Khaṭībī from Nasaf in Transoxania as chief *qāḍi* and gave the control of the congregational mosque to the Ḥanafites, even though the town was predominantly Shāfiʿite and traditionalist. Both Isfahan and Hamadan, where there had been few Ḥanafites immediately before the Saljūq age, as residential towns of the Saljūq sultans came to harbor sizable Ḥanafite communities. In Baghdad the Shāfiʿite chief *qāḍi* Ibn Mākūlā died shortly after Ṭughril-beg's first arrival and was replaced, through the intervention of the sultan's vizier al-Kundurī, by the Ḥanafite Abū ʿAbd Allāh al-Dāmaghānī.

While these measures in favor of Ḥanafism, which happened to be mostly detrimental to the interests of the Shāfiʿites, could be considered to be within the ruler's privilege to give preference to a particular rite for official occasions, Ṭughril-beg eventually went further to openly curbing the Shāfiʿites. In 445/1053, two years before his entry in Baghdad, he issued the order to curse al-Ashʿarī from the pulpits in Khurasan. The Ashʿarī accounts of this affair usually try to put the responsibility for the order on Ṭughril-beg's vizier ʿAmīd al-Mulk al-Kundurī, who is accused of Muʿtazilī and Shīʿī sympathies. From an open letter in defense of al-Ashʿarī written by Abu l-Qāsim al-Qushayrī, one of the victims of the ensuing persecution of Ashʿarites in Nishapur, it is clear, however, that the sultan stood squarely behind the measure. In the face of Shāfiʿite resistance, he ordered the arrest and deportation of the four most prominent Shāfiʿites. Abu l-Maʿālī al-Juwaynī, the leading Ashʿarī theologian, fled to Baghdad and later found refuge in Mekka and Medina. Ṭughril-beg replaced the Shāfiʿite *raʾīs,* the representative head of the town, by a member of the Ḥanafite Ṣāʿidī family giving him the title *raʾīs al-ruʾasāʾ*. Besides the Ashʿarīs, the Karrāmiyya and the Shīʿa (*rāfiḍa*), who constituted the other two large Muslim communities in Nishapur, were also officially cursed as innovators. Yet while at least one of the heretical doctrines with which al-Ashʿarī was charged was even more characteristic of Muʿtazilī teaching, there is no evidence that the Muʿtazila, who were generally Ḥanafites, were accused of heresy.

The persecution of the Ashʿarīs ended only after the death of Ṭughril-beg in 455/1063. His successor Alp Arslan replaced the vizier al-Kundurī with the staunchly Shāfiʿite Niẓām al-Mulk. In Nishapur Abū ʿAlī al-Manīʿī, a wealthy patron of the Shāfiʿites, was now appointed *raʾīs* of the town and was given permission to build a second congregational mosque where the Shāfiʿites could follow their own ritual. Al-Juwaynī was able to return to his home town. Alp Arslan thus consented to compensate the Shāfiʿites for the damage they had suffered without, however, taking away from the Ḥanafites their newly gained control of the old congregational mosque. Sultan Alp Arslan is described by his vizier Niẓām al-Mulk in his *Siyāsatnāma* as a fanatical Ḥanafite with a strong bias against Shāfiʿism who on various occasions expressed his displeasure at having a Shāfiʿite vizier. Niẓam al-Mulk confesses to have been in constant fear in this regard. This worry about the latent anti-Shāfiʿite prejudice of his master evidently induced Niẓām al-Mulk to proceed cautiously in his support for Ashʿarism during his sultanate. Only under Alp Arslan's successor Malikshāh would he feel confident enough to surround himself with Ashʿarites and show more openly his political backing of their cause.

In the *Siyāsatnāma,* his Book on Government, Niẓām al-Mulk pleaded his defense of Shāfiʿism. He argued repeatedly that there were in all the world only two good doctrinal schools following the right path, those of Abū Ḥanīfa and al-Shāfiʿī. While the Turks were all pure Muslims of the Ḥanafite rite, viziers, secretaries, administrators, and tax collectors should be taken only from Khurasanians belonging to either of these two schools since they were orthodox like the Turks. ʿIraqi secretaries should not be allowed to put their pens to paper since most of them belonged to heretical sects and would strive to undermine the Turkish interests. Niẓām al-Mulk's valiant efforts to gain the Shāfiʿites officially equal status with the Ḥanafites and to restore some of their lost privileges did not permanently influence Saljūq government. The late Saljūq historian Rāwandī, a fanatical Ḥanafite, reports that the vizier Abū Naṣr Aḥmad Niẓām al-Mulk (in office 500–504/1107–1111), son of the author of the *Siyāsatnāma,* "because of his bias (*taʿaṣṣub*)" for the Shāfiʿites tried to turn the congregational mosque of Isfahan over to them. The Saljūq sultan Muḥammad Tapar immediately ordered "heads to be chopped off" and sent troops to the town to ensure that the Ḥanafite chief *qāḍi* would pronounce the sermon in the mosque. There are reports of new severe measures against the Ashʿarīs under Muḥammad's son sultan Masʿūd. When he entered Ray in 537/1142–1143, the two most prominent Shāfiʿite scholars of the town, Abū Saʿīd b. al-Wazzān and Abu l-Faḍāʾil b. al-Mashshāṭ, were forced in his presence to sign documents repudiating their Ashʿarī doctrines and cursing al-Ashʿarī. In the following year he came to Baghdad accompanied by a Ḥanafite scholar, al-Ḥasan b. Abī Bakr al-Nīsābūrī, who with official support cursed al-Ashᶜarī from the pulpits of the mosque of the caliph's palace and the mosque of al-Manṣūr, the stronghold of the Ḥanbalites. At the instigation of ᶜAlī b. al-Ḥusayn, a Ḥanafite preacher popular with the Turks and patronized by sultan Malikshāh's daughter ᶜIṣmat Khātūn, sultan Masᶜūd ordered the deportation of the Shāfiᶜite Ashᶜarī preacher and Sufi Abu l-Futūḥ al-Isfarāyīnī. Two years later anti-Ashᶜarī tenets were officially sanctioned and announced in Hamadan in the presence of sultan Masᶜūd and his nephews Muḥammadshāh and Malikshāh. From Hamadan sultan Masᶜūd sent the Ḥanafite Abū Naṣr al-Hisanjānī to Baghdad to proclaim these doctrines in the mosques and *madrasa*s and to take the signatures of the scholars endorsing them. Next al-Hisanjānī went to Isfahan where his activities provoked riots which were suppressed by force. At this time the Khujandī family, the traditional leaders of the Shāfiᶜite community of Isfahan, seems to have run into trouble. Later al-Hisanjānī proclaimed the anti-Ashᶜarī tenets also in the mosque of Qazvin, then a stronghold of Shāfiᶜism. This anti-Shāfiᶜite bias was not just a whim of some Saljūq sultans. It was backed by the Ḥanafite fanaticism of the common Turkish soldiers. The Shiᶜite polemicist ᶜAbd al-Jalīl al-Rāzī writing around 565/1170 in Ray, to whom we owe much of the information on sultan Masᶜūd's anti-Ashᶜarī measures, could remind the Shāfiᶜites that if one of them would be questioned by a Turk in the market or the army camp concerning his beliefs he certainly would not dare confess his Ashᶜarism but would have recourse to *taqiyya,* precautionary dissimulation.

The disruption of the established balance between the two major Sunnite legal schools in Iran caused by the Saljūq invasion thus provoked unprecedented factional antagonism between them which could erupt in violence on the flimsiest occasion. In Marw the Shāfiᶜite and Ḥanafite communities already in the time of al-Maqdisī had separate congregational mosques. When Abu l-Muẓaffar Manṣūr al-Samᶜānī, who belonged to a well-known Ḥanafite family in the town and was himself a distinguished Ḥanafite scholar, announced his conversion to Shāfiᶜism in 468/1075, the Ḥanafite community was dismayed, and fighting broke out with the Shāfiᶜites. The Shāfiᶜites were forced to close their mosque and were prevented from holding the Friday prayer. The Ḥanafites, moreover, complained to the governor who was at the time absent in Balkh. He took their side and sent orders to Marw to put pressure on al-Samᶜānī to recant. The latter refused and was forced to leave the city. The Shāfiᶜites in Ṭūs and Nishapur gave him a hero's welcome, and the vizier Niẓām al-Mulk sent him robes of honor and money. He was given a place to teach in Nishapur. Only eleven years later he returned to his hometown and taught in the Shāfiᶜite *madrasa* there. His brother Abu l-Qāsim continued to reproach him and avoided him for a long time. Eventually he accepted his excuses. In 596/1200 Niẓām al-Mulk Masᶜūd b. ᶜAlī, vizier of the Khwārazmshāh Tekesh and patron of the Shāfiᶜites, built a mosque for the Shāfiᶜite community in Marw which surpassed the Ḥanafite mosque in height. The Ḥanafites, led by the *raᵓīs* Shaykh al-Islām, burnt it down, causing rioting to ensue between the two factions. When, on the other hand, the Shāfiᶜite *qāḍī* of Sāwa, ᶜUmdat al-Dīn Muḥammad b. ᶜAbd al-Razzāq (d. 561/1166) converted to the Ḥanafite school, he was accused by the Shāfiᶜites of acting merely out of fear and ambition trying to ingratiate himself with the officials of the Saljūq sultan.

While the factional strife could be kept under control by powerful government in the early Saljūq age, intercommunal warfare and rioting became widespread with the decline of the sultanate in later Saljūq and post-Saljūq times. Extensive destruction hit the major towns in Iran. The geographer Yāqūt describes the devastation caused in Isfahan by the recurrent fighting and pillaging between Shāfiᶜites and Ḥanafites. "Each time one faction gained the upper hand it plundered, burnt, and ruined the quarter of the other." Since sultan Masᶜūd antagonized the Shāfiᶜite community by his ostensibly anti-Ashᶜarī measures, the amīr Būzābeh in his revolt against him could rely on Shāfiᶜite support. The Shāfiᶜite *raᵓīs* of Isfahan, Ṣadr al-Dīn Abū Bakr Muḥammad b. ᶜAbd al-Laṭīf al-Khujandī, opened the gates at Būzābeh's approach in 542/1147. After the defeat and death of Būzābeh a year later, sultan Masᶜūd's governor of Isfahan, Rashīd al-Ghiyāthī, whom the Shāfiᶜite historian ᶜImād al-Dīn al-Iṣfahānī accuses of partisan bias against the Shāfiᶜites, hastened to punish those who had cooperated with the rebel. Abū Bakr al-Khujandī and his brother Maḥmūd fled in time, but the mob, presumably the Ḥanafites, plundered his *madrasa* and burnt its library. Sultan Masᶜūd soon afterwards pardoned the Khujandī brothers. When Abū Bakr, however, died in 552/1157, violent riots broke out between the Ḥanafites and Shāfiᶜites. In 560/1165 Ibn al-Athīr records fierce fighting lasting eight days between Ṣadr al-Dīn ᶜAbd al-Laṭīf, the son of Abū Bakr al-Khujandī, and other "leaders of the *madhhabs*," that is evidently again the Shāfiᶜites and the Ḥanafites. Many people were killed, and houses and markets were burnt or destroyed.

Yāqūt describes the ruin of Ray observed by himself reporting that he was told by an inhabitant that it was caused by the factional fighting, first between the Sunnites and the Shiʿites, and then between the Shāfiʿites and Ḥanafites. Zakariyyāʾ al-Qazwīnī speaks of the fanatical partisan spirit of the Ḥanafites and the Shāfiʿites in Ray leading to numerous battles between them in which the Shāfiʿites, despite being outnumbered by their opponents, always gained the upper hand.

In Nishapur the situation was not better. The author of the *Akhbār al-dawla al-Saljūqiyya* mentions an outbreak of fighting between the religious factions in the time of sultan Sanjar before 548/1153 in which seventy Ḥanafites were killed. Sanjar apparently intended to banish the leading Shāfiʿite scholar, Muḥyi l-Dīn Muḥammad b. Yaḥyā b. Manṣūr, from the city as a punishment, but then changed his mind. In 553/1158 the Shāfiʿites used the occasion of their feuding with the Shiʿites to burn down the Ḥanafite Ṣandaliyya *madrasa*. The factional fighting, which originally had broken out between the Shiʿites and the Shāfiʿites and lasted three years, soon must have turned into warfare between the Shāfiʿites and Ḥanafites. For in the end, according to Ibn al-Athīr's report, eight Ḥanafite and seventeen Shāfiʿite *madrasa*s had been destroyed. The factional feuding thus had already reduced some of the major towns of Iran to ruin before the Mongols invaded the country to complete the devastation.

The expansion of the Turks during the Saljūq age throughout Iran and into Anatolia, Iraq, Syria, and Egypt resulted not only in a substantial spread and increase of Ḥanafism there, but also in the general prevalence of the eastern, especially Transoxanian Ḥanafite tradition. As they moved westward, the Turks regularly gave preference to Ḥanafite scholars of eastern origin over local ones. Eastern, occasionally Turkish, scholars were usually given the positions of social and political prestige. They were appointed *qāḍī*s, preachers, imams, and professors at the newly founded *madrasa*s in the major cities. The result was a steady stream of eastern Ḥanafite scholars migrating toward western Iran and the central provinces of Islam where they became the highly respected teachers of the following generations of Ḥanafite jurists and dignitaries. This westward movement of eastern Ḥanafite scholars continued long beyond the Saljūq age into the Mongol period. It remained strong throughout the seventh/thirteenth century and gradually tapered off in the eighth/fourteenth century. While it was initially encouraged by the high esteem on which the eastern scholars could count in the west, it was later evidently also fed by the devastation of their eastern home countries in the political upheavals there.

The prevalence of the eastern Ḥanafite tradition brought about a major shift in the development of scholastic theology in Sunnism. In the early centuries of Islam, Muʿtazilism had taken the lead in the elaboration of systematic theological thought. The rise of *kalām* schools like the Kullābiyya and Ashʿarism which endeavored to defend traditionalist doctrine with the rational methods of the Muʿtazila had not seriously affected this leadership. The Buwayhid age witnessed a resurgence of the Muʿtazila culminating in the teaching of Qāḍī ʿAbd al-Jabbār and his pupils in Ray. This resurgence provoked the traditionalist counteroffensive of repression in Baghdad under the caliphs al-Qādir and al-Qāʾim and the persecution of the Muʿtazila in Ray and elsewhere by Maḥmūd of Ghazna. The Ḥanafite sense of solidarity of the Saljūq Turks initially encouraged a limited revival of Muʿtazilī teaching in both Ray and Baghdad. In the long term, however, eastern Ḥanafism swept away the theological deviations of the western Ḥanafites, in particular Muʿtazilism. Māturīdī theology, originally the local doctrine of the school of Samarqand, which had remained virtually unknown in the west before the rise of the Saljūqs, became the universal doctrine of the Ḥanafites.

Muʿtazilism survived, outside the Shīʿa, only in Khwārazm. There it was reinvigorated in the first half of the sixth/twelfth century by the authority of al-Zamakhsharī, author of a highly popular Muʿtazilī Qurʾan commentary, and his contemporary Rukn al-Dīn Maḥmūd b. al-Malāḥimī (d. 536/1141), elaborator of the theological doctrine of the last Muʿtazilī school founded by Abu l-Ḥusayn al-Baṣrī in Baghdad a century earlier.[19] Khwārazmian Ḥanafites continued to adhere to Muʿtazilism at least until the early ninth/fifteenth century. The prominent Ḥanafite scholar ʿAbd al-Jabbār al-Khuwārazmī who accompanied Tīmūr to Syria and acted as an interpreter between him and Ibn Khaldūn was a Muʿtazilī. But the fate of the Muʿtazilī school in Sunnite Islam had been sealed by the Saljūq expansion.

19. See "The Theology of al-Zamakhsharī."

Sufism and the Karrāmiyya

Ascetic and mystical tendencies have manifested themselves in Islam from the age of the Prophet and have ever been common throughout the Muslim world. In the early time they were mostly expressed in an individualistic and unorganized manner. Later the name Sufism came to cover the major organized currents of asceticism and mysticism in Sunnite, and sometimes Shiʿite, Islam. In order to trace the origins of Sufism back to the beginnings of Islam, the historians of the movement included among its representatives many illustrious figures of the early generations of Muslims in whom they seemed to discover religious motives similar to their own. Sufi orders traced their chains of initiation (*silsila*) back to the Prophet. Whatever the individual merit of such retrospective inclusions in the movement, they rather tend to obscure the real lines of development of the classical Sufi institutions, practices, and doctrinal traditions.

The Sufi historians, on the other hand, excluded from their ranks the most important ascetic movement in Iran during the third/ninth to the sixth/twelfth centuries: the Karrāmiyya. By the fifth/eleventh century the Karrāmiyya were almost universally condemned as a heretical sect and the apologists of Sufism, itself often accused of unorthodox tendencies, could ill afford to associate with their cause. Opposition to the Karrāmiyya, however, had not always been so uncompromising. Although the founder, Abū ʿAbd Allāh Muḥammad b. Karrām (d. 255/869), a Persianized Arab from Sijistān, was twice imprisoned in Nishapur by the Ṭāhirid government and died in exile in Jerusalem, he left behind a stable and widespread following in Iran. There is mention of some early refutations of Ibn Karrām and his school, one by the Imāmī al-Faḍl b. Shādhān of Nishapur (d. 260/874), and another, more significantly, by a Ḥanafite scholar, Abū Bakr Muḥammad b. al-Yamān al-Samarqandī (d. 260/874). The Karrāmiyya were also charged with heresy in the *Sawād al-aʿẓam,* the Ḥanafite creed officially espoused under the Samanids since the late third/ninth century.[1] Yet in the fourth/tenth century there was little criticism of the Karrāmiyya. Abū Muṭīʿ Makḥūl al-Nasafī (d. 318/930), a respected Ḥanafite author and ancestor of distinguished Ḥanafite scholars, does not mention them in his heresiography *al-Radd ʿalā ahl al-bidaʿ wa l-ahwāʾ*. His repudiation of the world as evil and his disapproval of active struggle for livelihood suggest that he at least viewed

1. Concerning these refutations see J. van Ess, *Ungenutzte Texte zur Karrāmīya*, p. 75.

the movement with sympathy.[2] Abū Manṣūr al-Māturīdī (d. 332/944) ignores them in his *Kitāb al-Tawḥīd.* The traveler and geographer al-Maqdisī (writing ab. 375/985), representing a sound, if broadminded, Sunnite outlook, does not hesitate to attest to their orthodoxy in view of their general adherence to the legal school of Abū Ḥanīfa.[3]

The Karrāmiyya stood in fact close to the eastern Ḥanafite tradition in both legal and basic theological doctrine. This was only natural in view of the still unchallenged predominance of Ḥanafism in Iran during the first half of the third/ninth century when Ibn Karrām was active. In the law and ritual, the latter put forward views of his own in a number of specific questions but in general followed the teaching of Abū Ḥanīfa. The Karrāmiyya were therefore later occasionally considered a branch of Ḥanafism. The Shiʿite author Sayyid Murtaḍā b. Dāʿī (first half of the sixth/twelfth century) distinguishes between those Karrāmiyya who adhered to the legal doctrine of Ibn Karrām and those regularly following the Ḥanafite school doctrine. To the latter belonged in particular some in Ghūr and Sind.[4]

The Karrāmiyya upheld the basic Murjiʾite position on faith denying that acts were a constituent part of it. According to their mystical doctrine, the first confession of faith was made by all human souls when God, according to Qurʾan VII 172, questioned them before their birth. They were thus all born in the status of believers and remained so unless they apostatized and confessed unbelief.[5] In legal terms, the Karrāmiyya defined faith as affirmation (*iqrār*) with the tongue of the two testimonies of faith (*shahādatayn*) to the exclusion of belief (*taṣdīq*) in the heart. As al-Shahrastānī explains, this referred only to the legal status of the *muʾmin* in this world from which they distinguished his situation at the time of the recompense in the hereafter. The hypocrite *(munāfiq),* who verbally confesses faith in Islam while concealing unbelief, was thus in their view truly a believer in this world, yet he deserved eternal punishment in the hereafter.[6] The Karrāmī doctrine thus did not, as the omissive reports of other heresiographers suggest, entail an irrational extremist position,[7] but rather agreed in substance with the doctrine of Abū Ḥanīfa.

A good deal of Karrāmī theological doctrine was evidently formu-

2. van Ess, pp. 55–60.
3. Al-Maqdisī, p. 365.
4. "The Spread of Māturīdism and the Turks," p. 123, n. 36.
5. ʿAbd al-Qāhir al-Baghdādī, *al-Farq bayn al-firaq,* ed. Muḥ. Badr, pp. 211–212.
6. Al-Shahrastānī, pp. 84–85.
7. Al-Ashʿarī, *Maqālāt al-islāmiyyīn,* ed. H. Ritter, p. 141; al-Baghdādī, *al-Farq,* p. 212; al-Ḥākim al-Jushamī, quoted by van Ess, p. 27.

lated in anti-Muʿtazilī argument. The Karrāmiyya affirmed that all good and evil in this world occurred in accordance with the will and decree of God and that God created the acts of men. They specifically rejected the Muʿtazilī tenet that God is rationally obliged to act in accordance with the best interest (*aṣlaḥ*) of man and to facilitate his acceptance of faith through benevolent assistance (*luṭf*).[8] Some arguments of Muḥammad b. Karrām quoted by Ibn Dāʿī in which he seeks to prove the arbitrary and unreasonable character of God's creation, of the religious law and of rulings of the Prophet evidently belong in the context of this controversy.[9] The Karrāmiyya held, however, that human reason is able to discern some good and evil without revelation and that man is obliged to recognize the existence of God through reason.[10] Here, too, they appear influenced by eastern Ḥanafite tradition in contrast to the uncompromisingly anti-rational position of Sunnite traditionalism and Ashʿarism.

Like the traditionalists, however, the Karrāmiyya were concerned with defending the literal acceptance of the anthropomorphic imagery used in the Qurʾan and the *ḥadīth* against the metaphorical interpretations of the Muʿtazila and other *kalām* schools. The heresiographers report many details about their explanations of the Qurʾanic description of God's rising (*istiwāʾ*) above His throne, about their doctrine of His corporeality and of His being located in the direction of above. Their opponents were evidently often able to elicit naïve and compromising responses from their scholars, who are described as mostly unsophisticated and muddleheaded. Only Muḥammad b. al-Hayṣam (d. 409/1019), recognized by friend and foe as the most capable Karrāmī theologian, put their doctrine, according to al-Shahrastānī, on a reasonable basis relying on the traditionalist formula of "acceptance without questioning the how (*balkafa*)."[11]

Highly controversial was also Ibn Karrām's doctrine of incidents (*ḥawādith*) subsisting in the essence of God. It was evidently formulated to counter the Muʿtazilī concept of divine attributes. The Muʿtazila distinguished, in order to preserve the immutability of the divine essence, between attributes of essence which applied to God eternally and unalterably, like power and knowledge, and attributes of act which applied to Him only at times and were subject to change in accordance with His acts. Thus they held that the attribute of creation belonged

8. Al-Shahrastānī, p. 84.
9. See van Ess, pp. 13–17.
10. Al-Shahrastānī, p. 84.
11. Al-Shahrastānī, p. 84. On Ibn al-Hayṣam see van Ess, pp. 60ff.

to God only when He created the world and that He had not been a creator from eternity. They further maintained that the temporal attributes of act could not subsist in the divine essence and must therefore be located elsewhere. The divine attribute and act of creation (*khalq*) was in fact often simply identified with the created (*makhlūq*), a view also adopted by the Ashʿarīs. The relationship between the immutable God and His creation thus seemed most tenuous. The eastern Ḥanafites did not accept this distinction between eternal attributes of essence and temporal attributes of act. They maintained that the attributes of act, which they commonly combined into a single one of "bringing into existence (*takwīn*)," were equally eternal and subsisted in the essence of God even before He brought forth the creation. The attribute of bringing forth, *takwīn,* was distinct from what was brought forth, *mukawwan.*

Ibn Karrām evidently started out from this anti-Muʿtazilī basis insisting on the eternity of the divine attributes of act. He was impressed, however, by the Muʿtazilī argument that the eternity of the attribute of creation would necessarily entail the eternity of creation itself. He met this objection by defining these attributes as eternal power (*qudra*) to act. Thus God's *khāliqiyya,* or *khāliqūqiyya,*[12] was His eternal power to create, His *rāziqiyya,* or *rāziqūqiyya,* His eternal power to provide sustenance, and His *kalām,* or *qāʾiliyya,* signified His eternal power to speak (*qawl*). His acts, however, were incidents (*ḥawādith*) arising in the divine essence in time through His power. These incidents were defined by the Karrāmiyya as accidents (*aʿrāḍ*), not attributes (*ṣifāt*). God was eternally creator by His attribute of power to create, not by His actually creating (*khalq*) in time. The name of creator belongs to Him eternally, while the meaning (*maʿnā*) arose in His essence in time.[13] Every thing and every event in this world is brought forth and annihilated by such incidents arising in the divine essence. According to some Karrāmī scholars, many incidents were in fact necessary to bring into existence or to annihilate anything in the world.

The notion of temporal incidents or accidents in the essence of God was roundly condemned by all other schools of *kalām.* Under pressure of their attacks, many Karrāmī theologians came to affirm that these incidents, unlike accidents in created substances, were permanent and

12. So al-Ḥākim al-Jushamī, quoted by van Ess, p. 22; al-Shahrastāni, p. 82, gives *khāliqiyya.* Words of this form, *kayfūfiyya, aḥmūqiyya,* and *ḥaythūthiyya,* were used by Ibn Karrām in a passage of his *K. ʿadhāb al-qabr* as quoted by al-Baghdādī, *Farq,* p. 207. van Ess, p. 22, n. 66.

13. Al-Ḥākim al-Jushamī, quoted by van Ess, pp. 21–22.

indelible. Thus they attempted to avoid the admission of a succession (*taʿāqub*) of temporals inhering in God since this defined temporal bodies in the theory of the *kalām* theologians. In the judgment of al-Shahrastānī, Muḥammad b. al-Hayṣam had succeeded to repair reasonably all the confused doctrines of Ibn Karrām except for this one of God's being a substratum for incidents which proved irreparable. Yet it was one of the most horrendous of absurdities.[14] In contrast, Ibn Taymiyya, a theologian much opposed to traditional *kalām,* referred to the Karrāmī doctrine with distinct sympathy.[15] Although he did not expressly admit it and criticized the Karrāmiyya on a side issue, misrepresenting their doctrine,[16] his own position, derived from the teaching of the pious ancestors (*salaf*), agreed with that of the Karrāmiyya in substance if not in formulation. The pious ancestors, according to Ibn Taymiyya, had held that speech and other acts inevitably arise in the speaker or agent.[17] God's acts, including the Qurʾan,[18] were, he admitted, unquestionably temporal. God acts and speaks whenever He will. Yet God's attributes of perfection, like creation and speech, belong to Him from eternity.[19]

The Karrāmiyya, however, were not primarily a legal or theological school. Ibn Karrām was remembered by his followers above all as a pious ascetic, a worshipper (*ʿābid*), and a public preacher. He is described in numerous anecdotes practicing his exclusive reliance on God (*tawakkul*). This was based on his prohibition of striving for economic gain (*taḥrīm al-makāsib*) which he considered as preventing the worshipper from devotion to God.[20] The *taḥrīm al-makāsib* of the Karrāmiyya was specifically declared heretical in the official Sāmānid creed *al-Sawād al-aʿẓam.*[21] They were commonly nicknamed "the mortifyers" (*mutaqashshifa*) for their ascetic practices.

14. Al-Shahrastānī, p. 83.
15. See H. Laoust, *Essai sur les doctrines sociales et politiques de Takī-d-dīn Aḥmad b. Taimīya,* pp. 81 n. 1, 159, 170.
16. Ibn Taymiyya objects to their view that God did not act and speak from eternity. He misrepresents their doctrine stating that according to them God did not have the power (*qudra*) to act and speak until this power occurred in him without any cause necessitating it. See Ibn Taymiyya, *Majmūʿat al-rasāʾil wa l-masāʾil,* ed. Muḥ. Rashīd Riḍā, III, pp. 29–30, 44, 159. The Karrāmiyya rather affirmed that God's power to act and speak was eternal.
17. *Majmūʿa,* III, p. 28.
18. See "The Origins of the Controversy Concerning the Creation of the Koran," pp. 512ff.
19. *Majmūʿa,* III, pp. 44–45.
20. van Ess, pp. 30–32.
21. See the Arabic version, Istanbul 1304/1887, p. 27. In the Persian version, *Tarjuma-yi al-sawād al-aʿẓam,* ed. ʿAbd al-Ḥayy Ḥabībī, pp. 122, 186, other aspects of Karrāmī doctrine are criticized.

The Karrāmiyya represented an activist and ostensive asceticism. They wanted to influence others by their conduct to change their way of life and criticized their worldliness in their sermons. Their rise split the ascetic-mystical movement in Nishapur. In opposition to them arose the current known as the Malāmatiyya founded by Abū Ḥafṣ ᶜAmr b. Muslim al-Ḥaddād (d. 265/878), Ḥamdūn al-Qaṣṣār (d. 270/883), and Saᶜīd b. Ismāᶜīl al-Ḥayrī. The Malāmatiyya viewed their commitment to the mystical path as a strictly personal matter and held that those following it should hide their practice by outward conformance to society, or even by reprehensible worldly conduct.[22]

Many of Ibn Karrām's followers were new converts to Islam. He was active preaching the faith in the countryside of Nishapur. Still a century later, Isḥāq b. Maḥmashādh (d. 383/993), ancestor of the family leading the Karrāmiyya in Nishapur until the middle of the sixth/twelfth century,[23] is reported to have converted numerous Zoroastrians and *dhimmī*s in the region. Nishapur came to shelter a strong Karrāmī community with a distinct low-class character. The town always remained the leading center of Karrāmī scholarship, and Muḥammad b. al-Hayṣam, who came from a village near Herat, taught and died there. In Herat, Ghūr and Gharchistān, the province between Herat and Marwarrūdh, Ibn Karrām achieved his greatest missionary successes converting the native non-Muslims. The Karrāmiyya still predominated in Herat in the fifth/eleventh century, and smaller towns like Afshīn and Sūrmīn were solidly Karrāmī. Ibn Karrām also founded a community in Samarqand.[24] The Karrāmiyya in Transoxania must have been involved in the efforts to convert the Turks to Islam but were evidently not very successful, at least in the longer term.[25] The early Ghaznawids, Sebüktegīn (367/977–387/997) and Maḥmūd (388/998–421/1030) during the first part of his reign, gave

22. J. Chabbi, "Remarques sur le développement historique des mouvements ascétiques et mystiques au Khorasan," in *SI* XLVI, pp. 54ff.

23. See the genealogy and information on the family assembled by van Ess, *Ungenutzte Texte,* pp. 33–35. Two further members of the family are mentioned by al-Samᶜānī, *al-Taḥbīr,* II, p. 239: Abu l-Qāsim Maḥmashādh b. Muḥammad b. Maḥmashādh b. Abī Muḥammad b. Maḥmashādh al-ᶜAbdalī (before 470/1078–542/1147) and his son ᶜAbd al-ᶜAzīz. It is not clear how they are related to the family. Chronologically Abu l-Qāsim Maḥmashādh could well be a grandson of nr. 6 of the genealogy, Maḥmashādh b. Aḥmad. In this case nr. 5, Abu l-ᶜAbbās/Abū ᶜAbd Allāh Aḥmad, would have been known under still another *kunya,* Abū Muḥammad. The final Maḥmashādh of the lineage in any case refers probably to the ancestor (nr. 1) of the family. The *nisba* al-ᶜAbdalī was used to refer to adherents of the school of Abū ᶜAbd Allāh b. Karrām (al-Samᶜānī, *al-Ansāb,* s.v. al-ᶜAbdalī).

24. van Ess, p. 31.

25. "The Spread of Māturīdism and the Turks," p. 121, n. 32a.

official backing to the Karrāmiyya probably because of the movement's strength in the central provinces of their kingdom. The Saljūqs from the beginning favored Transoxanian Ḥanafism, and the Karrāmiyya were officially cursed together with the Ashᶜarīs and the Shiᶜites under Ṭughril-beg. Under the Qarakhānids the Karrāmiyya were persecuted in Transoxania.

The last years of his life Ibn Karrām was active in Jerusalem and after his death a thriving Karrāmī community remained there centered about his tomb. He also gained some followers in the mountains of Lebanon.[26] The movement, however, always remained predominantly Persian and failed to expand much outside the Iranian world. Al-Maqdisī, who furnishes most information about the spread of the Karrāmiyya in his time, mentions a quarter (*maḥalla*) of them in Fusṭāṭ in Egypt. In the east he notes Karrāmī communities, besides those already mentioned, in Khuttal, Jūzjān, Marwarrūdh, the valley of Farghāna, Biyār, Gorgan, and the mountains of Ṭabaristān. In Bayhaq a *madrasa* for the Karrāmiyya was built in 414/1023[27] and there was later in the fifth/eleventh century, as in Nishapur, fighting between the Karrāmiyya and the Shāfiᶜite and Ḥanafite communities.

The remarkable speed with which the Karrāmiyya initially spread and their success in maintaining the strength of the movement for over two centuries, in sharp contrast to other early ascetic-mystical currents, seem partly to be due to their organization. It has repeatedly been suggested that the Karrāmiyya introduced the institution of convents, *khānaqāh*s, and *madrasa*s in Islam.[28] The most impressive evidence for this is provided by al-Maqdisī who associates *khānaqāh*s regularly and almost exclusively with the Karrāmiyya.[29] It is clear that in his time only they maintained such convents on a wide scale. Communal life in these convents must have been the norm for the active members of the movement. This practice probably goes back to the time of the founder. There is mention of his *madrasa* in Herat.[30] In the mountains of Lebanon some 4,000 of his followers were described

26. van Ess, p. 31.
27. Ibn Funduq, *Tārīkh-i Bayhaq,* ed. A. Bahmanyār, pp. 194–195.
28. J. Ribera y Taragon first argued that the *khānaqāh*s of the Karrāmiyya were also teaching institutions and that the *madrasa* of the Sunnite legal schools developed out of them. See his "Origin del Colegio Nidami de Bagdad," in *Disertaciones y opúsculos,* I, pp. 379ff. See also J. Chabbi, "Kh̲ānḳāh," in *E.I.,* 2nd ed.
29. Only in Dabīl (Dvin) al-Maqdisī (p. 379) mentions a *khānaqāh* which may, or may not, have belonged to Sufis. See Chabbi, "Remarques," p. 44.
30. van Ess, p. 31.

as living in monasteries (*ṣawāmiʿ*).[31] These different names presumably refer here to basically the same institution. No details are known about the use and rules of the convents. Provided with endowments and the support of the larger communities, they allowed the residents to abstain from working for their livelihood, as prescribed by Ibn Karrām, and to devote their lives to the worship of God and preaching the truth to others. Given the theological and legal concerns of the movement, they must have often also served teaching needs. The clear institutional distinction between *khānaqāh* and *madrasa* did evidently not yet exist. The network of convents facilitated easy movement and spiritual interchange helping to maintain close bonds among the dispersed Karrāmī communities. The Karrāmiyya remained a single movement even though they lacked a common leadership. The subdivisions of the Karrāmiyya mentioned by the heresiographers were not sects but schools and currents which tolerated each other.

As the Karrāmiyya disintegrated in the sixth/twelfth century, Sufism developed into a popular mass movement. Persian Sufism was in this period closely associated with Shāfiʿism and Ashʿarism. Ibn-i Munawwar, the biographer of the Sufi Abū Saʿīd b. Abi l-Khayr writing between 574/1178 and 588/1192, went so far as to assert that all Sufi masters since the time of al-Shāfiʿī had been Shāfiʿites and that even those who originally adhered to another school adopted Shāfiʿite doctrine after God elected them for His friendship. The reason for this was, he explained, that the Sufis were deeply concerned with a meticulous and rigorous practice of the obligatory rites and devotions of Islam and even supererogatory acts in order to mortify their desires, and this attitude was most in harmony with the rigorism of Shāfiʿite law. Although Ibn-i Munawwar insisted that the Sufis would not discriminate between al-Shāfiʿī and Abū Ḥanīfa, both eminently pious imams, he clearly implied that Ḥanafism, the rationalist school (*aṣḥāb raʾy*) associated with the Muʿtazila who denied the miracles of Sufi saints, was unsuited for Sufis. Some people had claimed that Bāyazīd Basṭāmī, the famous Sufi living before the expansion of Shāfiʿism in Iran, had adopted the teaching of Abū Ḥanīfa but he, Ibn-i Munawwar claims anachronistically, rather practiced the doctrine of his teacher, the Shiʿite imam Jaʿfar al-Ṣādiq.[32]

31. Ibid. *Ṣawāmiʿ* probablay means here monasteries rather than cells. Otherwise it would have been difficult for a visitor passing through the region to meet more than 4,000 followers of Ibn Karrām.

32. Ibn-i Munawwar, *Asrār al-tawḥīd fī maqāmāt al-Shaykh Abī Saʿīd,* ed. Dh. Ṣafā, pp. 20–24.

While Ibn-i Munawwar is obviously biased and overlooks prominent early Sufis who were Ḥanafites, it is true that the Sufi movements in Iraq and Iran were since the fourth/tenth century predominantly Shāfiᶜite. Many of its leaders were fully trained Shāfiᶜite jurists and some of them Ashᶜarī theologians. The prominent apologists and popularizers of Sufism, who achieved the general recognition of its Sunnite orthodoxy, Abū Naṣr al-Sarrāj of Ṭūs (d. 378/988), al-Sulamī of Nishapur (d. 412/1021), Abū Nuᶜaym al-Iṣfahānī (d. 430/1038), al-Qushayrī of Nishapur (d. 465/1072), and al-Ghazālī of Ṭūs (d. 505/1111), were Shāfiᶜites, some of them with a strong anti-Ḥanafite bias. Exceptions were the eastern Ḥanafites al-Kalābādhī of Kalābādh near Bukhara (d. ar. 384/994), author of the *K. al-Taᶜarruf li-madhhab ahl al-taṣawwuf,* and Hujwīrī of Ghazna (d. ab. 469/1077). Al-Kalābādhī described the creed of the Sufis in terms of the Māturīdī theology prevalent in Transoxania but could not entirely conceal the traditionalist and Ashᶜarī foundation of their views. Shāfiᶜites were also the founders of the early Sufi orders in Iran and Iraq. While the close alliance of Sufism and Shāfiᶜism initially helped the former to gain acceptance in orthodox Sunnism, it later, as Sufism developed into a broad popular movement, furthered the spread of Shāfiᶜism in Iran at the expense of Ḥanafism.[33] The latter came more and more to be primarily identified with the Turks especially as the old centers of eastern Ḥanafism in Transoxania were progressively Turkicized.

Despite a growing sense of a common purpose and superregional solidarity, Sufism remained in the fourth/tenth century still largely unorganized and locally based. A group of Sufis would gather around a shaykh, but usually disperse soon after his death even if they remained devoted to his message. The twelve "sects" into which Hujwīrī divided the Sufis in his time were typical doctrinal currents, usually called after its founder, rather than organized groups. Few Sufis would in fact have been able to identify themselves fully and exclusively with any of these currents. The only one of the groups which, according to Hujwīrī, maintained the original teaching of its founder unchanged were the Sayyārīs, followers of Abu l-ᶜAbbās al-Qāsim al-Sayyārī of Marw (d. 342/953). He had been a disciple of the Iraqi Sufi Abū Bakr

33. Still in the eighth/fourteenth century the Kubrawī Sufi ᶜAlī al-Hamadānī converted from the Ḥanafī school to Shāfiᶜism after al-Shāfiᶜī appeared to him in a dream demanding that he follow the rites of the majority of Sufi shaykhs and after the Prophet, accompanied by Abū Ḥanīfa, had given him permission to do so in another dream. See M. Molé, "Les Kubrawiyya entre sunnisme et shiisme," in *REI,* XXVIII, pp. 113–114.

al-Wāsiṭī who came to teach in Marw. The school continued after al-Sayyārī's death under heads with sufficient authority to maintain doctrinal unity and attracted a numerous following in Marw, Nasā, and Bāward.[34] Nothing is known about its fate after Hujwīrī's time.

The first Sufi order in Iran, and indeed in Islam, was the Murshidiyya or Kāzarūniyya founded by Abū Isḥāq al-Kāzarūnī, known as Shaykh-i Murshid (352/963–426/1035). Al-Kāzarūnī came from a poor local family in Kāzarūn, west of Shiraz; his grandfather had still been a Zoroastrian. Like Ibn Karrām, he represented an activist asceticism, was a powerful preacher and converted numerous Zoroastrians to Islam. His strictures and aggressive conduct toward the non-Muslims brought him and his followers into sometimes violent conflict with the strong Zoroastrian community backed by the local Būyid authorities. He preached the *jihād* against the infidels, and groups of his followers carried out campaigns against the Christians in Anatolia.[35]

Al-Kāzarūnī was a Shāfiʿite and professed an orthodox Ashʿarī creed.[36] Rejecting the prohibition of striving for one's livelihood upheld by the Karrāmiyya, he advocated and practiced a moderate self-denial in respect to food, drink, and clothing. Its purpose was to weaken the carnal instincts of the soul and to orient the heart toward God. Particular importance was accorded to the regular practice of hospitality to travelers and charity toward the poor. The convents founded by al-Kāzarūnī and his followers functioned as hospices for strangers and were used for channeling material aid to the needy on an impressive scale. Al-Kāzarūnī received gifts from wealthy patrons to carry on this charity. The members of the order were required to live in the convents and spent much time in prayer, devotions, vigils, recitations of the Qurʾan, and some study of *ḥadīth,* besides their service to the convents and the poor. Otherwise there was no teaching, though members could get permission to travel in order to pursue religious studies. Al-Kāzarūnī showed no interest in the speculative theories and gnostic theosophy of Sufism and did not develop a specific method of spiritual training and exercises for the novices.

During his lifetime al-Kāzarūnī and his followers established sixty-five convents in villages and towns in western and southern Iran, including Zanjān, Isfahan, Fasā and Kirman. Unlike other Sufi shaykhs

34. Hujwiri, *The Kashf al-Maḥjūb,* trans. R. A. Nicholson, p. 251; F. Meier, *Abū Saʿīd-i Abu l-Hayr,* p. 443.

35. On al-Kāzarūnī see in general F. Meier, *Die Vita des Scheich Abū Isḥāq al-Kāzarūnī.*

36. Meier, *Die Vita,* pp. 24ff.

of the time, he maintained close control from Kāzarūn over these branches. Having no children of his own, he appointed before his death a close companion, Khaṭīb ʿAbd al-Karīm b. ʿAlī b. Saʿd as his successor in the leadership of the order. The next three successors belonged to the latter's family. The central leadership in Kāzarūn was thus maintained. The order spread later far outside Iran. Ibn Baṭṭūṭa (d. ab. 770/1369) mentions its agents in the harbors of India and China where they traded the *baraka* of the founder for vows of contributions by sea travelers worried about the safety of their passage. The money collected in this way constituted the order's main source of income. The order was also widespread then in Anatolia where it was known by the name of Isḥāqiyya.

Initially al-Kāzarūnī and his order found little recognition among Sufis, evidently since his primarily practical outlook and lack of gnostic teaching ran counter to the interests of mainstream Sufism. Hujwīrī refers to him only in passing among many others stating that he did not meet him. Anṣārī Harawī (d. 481/1089) does not mention him at all in his *Ṭabaqāt al-Ṣūfiyya.* Institutional success was evidently still not considered significant by most Sufis. Sufi shaykhs now often founded, and taught in, *khānaqāh*s and appointed successors to guide their disciples after their death. Their communities, however, remained local and usually did not survive long.

The development of Sufi orders made only little progress in Iran until after the Mongol conquest, although some of the key figures and founders of "paths" (*ṭarīqa*s) to whom the later orders adhered still lived in the pre-Mongol age. While several Sufi teachers of Persian origin established *ṭarīqa*s which became widespread chiefly outside Iran, two men in particular influenced, directly or indirectly, the developments in Iran and Transoxania. Concerning the biography of Abū Yaʿqūb Yūsuf b. Ayyūb al-Hamadānī (ca. 441/1049–535/1140), there exist two totally different accounts. According to the Shāfiʿite traditionist Abū Saʿd al-Samʿānī (d. 562/1167), who heard *ḥadīth* from him in Marw, he came in his youth from Būzanajird, a village near Hamadan, to Baghdad to study law and legal methodology under the famous Shāfiʿite scholar Abū Isḥāq al-Shīrāzī in the Niẓāmiyya *madrasa.* He also heard *ḥadīth* in various other towns, including Isfahan, Bukhara, and Samarqand. In his legal studies he succeeded brilliantly and became a favorite of his teacher, but then he abandoned them to devote himself to a life of asceticism, worship, and Sufi practice. He may well have been encouraged in this by al-Shīrāzī who seems to have had ties with Abū Isḥāq al-Kāzarūnī in his youth and himself inclined to an ascetic life. Yūsuf al-Hamadānī mentioned two Sufi shaykhs influencing and guiding him, ʿAbd Allāh al-Jūnī(?) and al-Simnānī, neither of whom can be definitely identified.[37] He later established a thriving *khānaqāh* in Marw and taught also in Herat for prolonged periods. Some time after he died in Bāmayīn, the main village of Bādhghīs, on his way from Herat to Marw, his body was transferred to Marw. His tomb there was still known centuries later.[38]

The other account is a hagiographical vita known as *Maqāmāt-i Yūsuf-i Hamadānī* or *Risāla-yi Ṣāḥibiyya* and was written after 600/1204 by, or in the name of, ʿAbd al-Khāliq b. ʿAbd al-Jamīl al-Ghujduwānī.[39] From ʿAbd al-Khāliq derives the line of affiliation of the Khwājagān, the forerunners of the Naqshbandiyya order. He was a Ḥanafite born in Ghujduwān, a village in the oasis of Bukhara, to parents who are said to have emigrated there from Malaṭya in Anatolia. In this account Yūsuf al-Hamadānī's lineage is traced to Abū Ḥanīfa, the founder of the legal school, and he is described as a fervent follower of his ancestor's doctrine. His creed, as given in the *Risāla-yi Ṣāḥibiyya,* agreed fully with that of the Transoxanian Ḥanafites and he expressly defined the orthodox faith of the Muslim community (*jamāʿat*) as identical with the teaching of Abū Ḥanīfa and his companions. Instead of the two obscure shaykhs named by al-Hamadānī himself, the account describes Abū ʿAlī al-Fārmadhī of Ṭūs, a famous mystic who also guided al-Ghazālī, as his Sufi master. Born already in 320/1029, al-Hamadānī moved from Hamadān together with eleven companions, among them al-Ghujduwānī, to Samarqand. He was present there long before 504/111 and taught in a *khānaqāh.* Before his death in Samarqand he named his four successors to al-Ghujduwānī, who was the fourth one of them.

This hagiographical vita of Yūsuf al-Hamadānī must be considered

37. In the biography of Yūsuf al-Hamadānī contained in the abridgment of al-Samʿānī's *Dhayl Taʾrīkh Baghdād,* ms. Leiden Or 29(2), the name of the first shaykh is given as ʿAbd Allāh al-Jūnī. In the edition of Ibn al-Jawzī's *al-Muntaẓam* (X 94) it appears as ʿAbd Allāh al-Jawshanī, and in his *Ṣifat al-ṣafwa* (IV 61) as ʿAbd Allāh al-Khūnī. Al-Dhahabī, quoting al-Hamadānī on the authority of al-Samʿānī, gives the name of the other shaykh as *fulān* al-Simnānī (*Siyar al-nubalāʾ,* XX 68). Jāmī identified the two as Abū ʿAbd Allāh (Muḥammad b. Ḥamūya) Juwaynī, the ancestor of the famous Sufi family, Banū Ḥamūya, originating from Juwayn and Ḥasan (al-Sakkāk) Simnānī (*Nafaḥāt al-uns,* pp. 375, 414). This identification appears to be entirely conjectural and most likely mistaken.

38. See Jāmī, *Nafaḥāt,* p. 375. Al-Samʿānī and Ibn al-Najjār's vitas of al-Hamadānī are best preserved in al-Dhahabī, *Siyar al-nubalāʾ,* XX 66–69 and Ibn Khallikān, *Wafayāt al-aʿyān,* ed. I. ʿAbbās, III 78–80.

39. The *Risāla-yi Ṣāḥibiyya* has been published by Saʿīd Nafīsī in *Farhang-i Īrān Zamīn* I/1, pp. 70–101.

entirely fictitious. Its data are both chronologically impossible and incompatible with those provided by al-Hamadānī's pupil al-Samʿānī. The latter could, moreover, hardly have failed to note if al-Hamadānī had ever abandoned the Shāfiʿite school of his teacher al-Shīrāzī and had joined that of Abū Ḥanīfa. Rather is it known that when he returned for a visit to Baghdad in 506/1112, long after his conversion to Sufism, he taught *ḥadīth* and preached in the Niẓāmiyya, the citadel of Shāfiʿism in Baghdad and received great public applause. It is highly unlikely that al-Ghujduwānī was ever his disciple if he wrote after 600/1204 and died as late as 617/1220, as some sources state.

The vita thus was written to provide a foundation legend for the movement of the Khwājagān affiliating them with a highly reputed and widely respected Sufi shaykh. The need for such a legend must have been acutely felt in the case of this Transoxanian order whose strongly Ḥanafite foundation signified a major deviation from the predominant association of Sufism with Shāfiʿism. The real founder of the Khwājagān was al-Ghujduwānī who also formulated the eight principles of exercise of the *ṭarīqa* which were later expanded to eleven by Bahāʾ al-Dīn al-Naqshabandī (d. 791/1389) after whom the Naqshbandiyya were called. Centered in Bukhara, the Khwājagān-Naqshbandiyya became a traditionally Ḥanafite, strictly Sunnite, and urban-based order. It later spread widely throughout Central Asia, India, Kurdistan, Anatolia, and Syria.

Another Transoxanian affiliation claiming to derive from Yūsuf al-Hamadānī was that of the Yasawiyya. Aḥmad al-Yasawī (d. 562/1146) was a Turkish Sufi from Yasī in Turkistan and is said to have become a disciple of al-Hamadānī in Bukhara or Samarqand. In the *Risāla-yi Ṣāḥibiyya* he is mentioned as the third successor (*khalīfa*) appointed by the master. He returned, however, to Turkistan to guide his own followers there and thus became the founder of an affiliation separate from the Khwājagān. Although there are no chronological obstacles to his having met al-Hamadānī, the latter's influence on him was hardly more meaningful than on al-Ghujduwānī. The Yasawiyya became a widespread Sufi tradition among the Turks from eastern Turkistan to Anatolia. They were mostly itinerant with few fixed centers except the tombs of some of their shaykhs. Amalgamating Ḥanafism with popular Turkish traditions, and open to heterodox influences, they were active chiefly among the Turcoman nomads and in the countryside. From them sprang the Bektāshiyya order in which heretical doctrines of an extremist Shiʿite, rather than Imāmī, type were most manifest.

While the Yasawiyya and even the Khwājagān-Naqshbandiyya affected Iran proper only marginally, the Kubrawiyya, although originating in a marginal province, Khwārazm, developed into a major Sufi movement in Khurasan and expanded, with its branches, through much of the country, besides Central Asia and India. Najm al-Dīn Kubrā, from whom the Kubrawiyya derive, was born in 540/1145–1146 in Khīwa, a Shāfiʿite enclave in otherwise predominantly Ḥanafite Muʿtazilī Khwārazm. Like Yūsuf al-Hamadānī, Kubrā himself was a Shāfiʿite and traveled widely in order to hear *ḥadīth* in Nishapur, Hamadan, Mekka, and Alexandria. At the same time he took an interest in mysticism and eventually decided to enter the Sufi path. His masters were Rūzbihān al-Fārisī in Cairo, Ismāʿīl al-Qaṣrī in Dizfūl, and ʿAmmār al-Bidlīsī in Bidlīs, who seems to have influenced him most deeply. Later he returned to Khwārazm and taught there until his death at the hands of the Mongol conquerors in 618/1221.[40]

Kubrā's mystical teaching, as it is expressed in his writings, represents a moderate theosophy based on a generally orthodox Islamic foundation, remote from the speculative Sufism and mystical monism of his contemporary Ibn al-ʿArabī (d. 638/1240). He was the first Sufi to describe in detail the visual and auditory phenomena experienced by the mystics and to discuss their significance. The *unio mystica* was described by him as an identification with the divine attributes and with the divine essence or a gradual vanishing (*fanāʾ*) of the self of the mystic in them. While moderate Sufis in the past had maintained that the evanescence in the divine attributes occurs only in the consciousness of the mystic and does not imply an actual loss of his own attributes, Kubrā held the substitution of the divine attributes for the human ones to be real. There was some contemporary muted criticism that his doctrine implied *ittiḥād,* union of the mystic with God, although he avoided using the term. Altogether, however, his Sunnite orthodoxy was not questioned.[41]

Kubrā's Sunnism evidently was not compromised either by his quotations of some pro-ʿAlid *ḥadīth*s and his expressions of reverence toward ʿAlī, Fāṭima and their descendants. These did not go beyond the practice of earlier Sufis and were balanced by expressions of reverence for the caliphs preceding ʿAlī, for ʿĀʾisha, and other Companions.[42] There is certainly no basis for the claim of some late Imāmī

40. On Najm al-Dīn Kubrā see especially F. Meier, *Die Fawāʾiḥ al-Ǧamāl wa-Fawātiḥ al-Ǧalāl des Naǧm ad-Dīn al-Kubrā.*

41. See the judgment of al-Dhahabī (Shams al-Dīn) quoted in al-Ṣafadī, *al-Wāfī bi l-wafayāt,* VII, p. 263.

42. Meier, *Die Fawāʾiḥ,* pp. 62–64; Molé, pp. 71–74.

authors that he was a Shiᶜite. Pro-ᶜĀlid tendencies and, at a later stage, extremist Shiᶜite ideas became, however, common among the leaders of the Persian Kubrawiyya. These developments came to a head when Sayyid Muḥammad Nūrbakhsh, a Shiᶜite whose father had emigrated from al-Aḥsā in eastern Arabia to Khurasan, succeeded to the leadership in ab. 826/1423. Nūrbakhsh claimed to be the Expected Imam and the Mahdī. Although he exalted the sanctity of the Twelve Imams, he expressly repudiated the Imāmī dogma confining the number of imams to twelve and denied that the Twelfth Imam could physically return. His teaching was partly based on Imāmī doctrine but transformed it into Sufi thought. In concord with the earlier masters of the Kubrawiyya he appealed to the ideal unity of Islam embodied in Sufism which alone embraced the totality of the faith and could overcome all sectarian divisions. At the same time the Kubrawiyya was rent by a schism as a section refused to recognize the leadership of Nūrbakhsh and accepted ᶜAbd Allāh Barzishābādī as their shaykh. Both branches continued as separate orders and became predominantly Shiᶜite. In the later Safavid age the remaining followers of Nūrbakhsh were absorbed by the other branch, now known as the Dhahabiyya. The latter is one of the Shiᶜite orders still active today.

The gradual evolution of the Kubrawiyya toward Shiᶜism was no isolated phenomenon in the Mongol and Timurid age. Philo-ᶜAlid and Shiᶜite tendencies became increasingly apparent in Sufi movements active among Persians and Turcomans in Iran and Anatolia. The close ties which had bound Sufism to Shāfiᶜite Sunnism in the pre-Mongol age gave way to universalist claims which readily accommodated and absorbed Shiᶜite elements. Most often such elements were related to popular and extremist forms of Shiᶜism rather than orthodox Imāmī Shiᶜism. There is little evidence that the spread of Imāmī Shiᶜism was substantially furthered by this development at the time. It did, however, prepare the ground for the conversion of Iran to Imamism in the Safavid age.

Khārijism: The ᶜAjārida and the Ibāḍiyya

Khārijism, the schismatic revolutionary movement arising out of the opposition in ᶜAlī's Kufan army to his arbitration agreement with Muᶜāwiya after the battle of Ṣiffīn (37/657), came to affect Iran from an early date. Its motivation was, as has been emphasized by J. Wellhausen,[1] essentially Islamic rather than Arab. The Khārijites were fanatically uncompromising in their application of the theocratic principle of Islam expressed in their slogan *la ḥukma illā li llāh,* "rule belongs to God alone." Even the caliphs, in their opinion, must unconditionally submit to this rule as embodied in the Qurʾan. If they fail to do so, like ᶜUthmān, ᶜAlī, and Muᶜāwiya, they must be called to repent and on refusal be removed by force, whatever their previous merits in Islam. Those who backed them or failed to dissociate from them openly must equally be fought without relent. It was only consistent with their theocratic motivation that they repudiated the exclusive right of the Quraysh to hold the caliphate, in spite of their admiration for Abū Bakr and ᶜUmar, and maintained that any meritorious Muslim, even a black slave, could be chosen as the legitimate imam and Commander of the Faithful. As a heresiographer of the third/ninth century put it, "all Khārijites claim that the imam may be of any race of the Arabs and the non-Arabs, without distinction in their view. They hold that boasting about races (*al-iftikhār bi l-ajnās*) and giving preference to one over the other is unbelief (*kufr*). The only basis for preference in their view is piety (*taqwā*)."[2]

Wellhausen's view of the character of early Khārijism must seem still valid as against more recent interpretations portraying a Bedouin Arab motivation of the early Khārijites who, it is suggested, tried to reconstitute their egalitarian tribal structure on an Islamic basis and formed "charismatic small sect-communities" or "communities of saints" guaranteeing salvation to its members.[3] It is true that the Khā-

1. *Die religiös-politischen Oppositionsparteien im alten Islam,* pp. 11–17.
2. Al-Nāshiʾ, *Masāʾil al-imāma,* p. 68.
3. This view has been developed by W. M. Watt, especially in his "Khārijite Thought in the Umayyad Period," pp. 215–231. See also his *The Formative Period of Islamic Thought,* pp. 34–37. It has been accepted by C. E. Bosworth, *Sīstān under the Arabs,* pp. 37–39. It is to be noted that neither Brünnow nor Wellhausen suggested that, "The *mawlā* elements of Basra and Lower Iraq were the most fertile recruiting-grounds for the first Khawārij" as Bosworth (p. 38) states. Brünnow considered the early Khārijites as Arab bedouins giving free rein to their anarchic instincts, whereas Wellhausen, while not denying their Arab bedouin origins, maintained that with their settlement in the Muslim garrison towns they had abandoned the bedouin way of life and adopted a primarily Islamic motivation.

rijites had a strong communal spirit and put great store on belonging to the "saved community (*firqa nājiya*)." It was they who first adopted, and ever refined in their theological discussions, the religious principle of *walāya* and *barāʾa,* associating in solidarity with those whom they considered as the people of Paradise and dissociating from "the people of Hell." However, it was not membership in a community, but strict adherence to the *dīn* owed to God, religious tenets and conduct, which guaranteed salvation. If the community, or its leader, even slightly deviated in their view from the right conduct enjoined by *dīn,* they were ever ready to dissociate from it and to form a separate community. This primary insistence on right conduct rather than on communal solidarity led to the extreme factionalism of the Khārijite movement. The concept of a "charismatic community" is valid for the *jamāʿa* of Sunnism but inappropriate for Khārijism.[4] Defining *dīn* and *jamāʿa* as the two poles of the Islamic theocracy, Wellhausen rightly observed: "In the conflict between *dīn* and *jamāʿa,* between the duty to put God and the Law above everything else and the duty to stay with the community and obey the imam, the Khārijites ranged themselves resolutely on the side of *dīn.*"[5]

The "egalitarianism" of the Khārijites was of a different kind than that of the bedouin tribes. The imam of the Khārijites was to be chosen only on the basis of religious merit and suitability, not on any privilege of blood relationship. To obey all his orders was an indisputable religious duty as long as he did not deviate from his religious duties. Chieftainship in bedouin tribes was strictly defined by blood relationship and membership in the established leading family; only within these limits could it be based on personal merit.[6] The egalitarianism of the bedouins rather reflected the lack of power of the chief whose authority rested more on his ability to persuade than on a right to command.

The Islamic egalitarianism of the Khārijites soon attracted non-Arab *mawālī* to their fold. Already in 38/658, a year after Ṣiffīn, there

4. The charismatic character of the Sunnite *jamāʿa* has been pointed out by Watt (*Formative Period,* p. 36). The Sunnite concept, however, was not derived from a Khārijite precedent, as he suggested, but rather developed against the Khārijite and Shiʿite opposition. The charismatic character of the *jamāʿa* is most clearly reflected in well-known Sunnite *ḥadīths* like: "My community will never agree on an error," and: "Whoever removes himself from the Community by the space of a single span withdraws his neck from the halter of Islam," whose anti-Khārijite tendency is evident.

5. *Oppositionsparteien,* p. 14.

6. "With true nomadic egalitarianism the leader (sc. of the Khārijites) might be chosen from any tribe, or might even be a non-Arab," Watt, *Formative Period,* p. 37. Nothing could in fact be more remote from nomadic egalitarianism.

is mention of a group of 200 or 400 Kufan Khārijites led by the Arab Abū Maryam of Saʿd Tamīm who were nearly exclusively *mawālī*. They assembled at Shahrazūr and approached Kufa with great bravery before they were killed by ʿAlī's followers, except for some fifty who asked for pardon.[7] Under Muʿāwiya's governor al-Mughīra b. Shuʿba (41–ca. 50/661–670), Abū ʿAlī, a Kufan *mawlā* of the Banu l-Ḥārith b. Kaʿb, revolted with a group of Khārijite *mawāli*. When warned by the leader of the army against them that the Arabs would fight them for the sake of the faith, they answered: "We have heard a wonderful Qurʾan which guides to the right path. We put our faith in it and shall not associate any partner with our Lord (Qurʾan LXXII 1–2). God has sent our prophet to all the people and did not withhold him from anyone." They were killed in the ensuing battle.[8]

In this early period, Khārijite refugees from Kufa and Basra carried their cause into Iranian territory. Ḥayyān b. Ẓabyān al-Sulamī, a Kufan Khārijite wounded in the battle of al-Nahrawān, escaped with some ten companions to Ray and stayed there until the murder of ʿAlī (40/661) when he returned to Kufa.[9] When he later in 58/678 rose in revolt there is mention of partisans of his in Ray and the mountains.[10] In 46/666, after Ziyād b. Abīhi had come as governor to Basra, the Khārijite Sahm b. Ghālib al-Hujaymī left for Ahwaz where he stirred up a rebellion.[11] It was during the turbulent conditions of the Second Civil War, however, that Khārijism became firmly implanted in Iran. Two large groups of Khārijites were driven to seek refuge in the southern provinces of the country, the Azāriqa from Basra and the ʿAṭawiyya from Arabia.

The Azāriqa were the most radical Khārijite sect. They held the killing of the women and children of non-Khārijite Muslims licit and considered as polytheists (*mushrikūn*) even those Khārijites who would not join their rebellion and emigrate to their army camp, which they called, in analogy to Medina in the time of Muḥammad, their abode of emigration (*dār hijra*). The rest of the Muslim world was in their eyes an abode of infidelity (*dār kufr*) and of polytheism. There could

7. Ibn al-Athīr, III, pp. 314–315. There were only six Arabs including Abū Maryam among them. The revolt of Abū Maryam is mentioned also in other sources (al-Ashʿarī, *maqālāt*, pp. 130–131; al-Baghdādī, *al-Farq*, p. 61), but without notice of his non-Arab following.

8. Al-Yaʿqūbī, *Taʾrīkh*, II, p. 262. Al-Yaʿqūbī describes this as the first rising of the *mawālī*.

9. Al-Ṭabarī, II, pp. 17–18.

10. Al-Ṭabarī, II, p. 182.

11. Al-Ṭabarī, II, p. 83.

be no state of peace between the realms. The Azāriqa, among whom tribesmen of Tamīm were initially predominant, entered Ahvaz under their first leader, Nāfiʿ b. al-Azraq, in 64/684 and since 66/686 established themselves in Fars and Kirman, now led by al-Zubayr b. Māḥūz (66–69/686–688) and Qaṭarī b. Fujāʾa (69/688–ca. 79/698). Coins minted in the name of Qaṭarī with the title Commander of the Faithful in several towns of Fars in the years 69/688–689 and 75/694–695 indicate his firm hold on the province.[12]

The ʿAṭawiyya, named after their leader ʿAṭiyya b. al-Aswad al-Ḥanafī, were a branch of the Najadāt, followers of Najda b. ʿĀmir, who in the time of the caliphate of ʿAbd Allāh b. al-Zubayr seized large parts of the Arabian peninsula. The Najadāt repudiated some of the more extreme views of Nāfiʿ b. al-Azraq. They did not permit the killing of the women and children of their Muslim opponents but captured and enslaved them. The Khārijites who failed to join their fight were considered by them merely as hypocrites (*munāfiqūn*) and thus could not be killed. They held that there could be times when revolutionary activity must lapse and it was permissible to conceal their beliefs and practice *taqiyya,* religious dissimulation.[13] ʿAṭiyya and his followers, mostly of the tribe of Ḥanīfa, left Arabia in 72/691 for Kirman which had earlier been a base of the followers of Qaṭarī.[14] Coins in the name of ʿAṭiyya b. al-Aswad struck in Kirman are known from the years 72–75/691–695 and perhaps 76/695–696.[15] Although ʿAṭiyya did not claim the title of Commander of the Faithful on his issue, he and Qaṭarī were obviously rivals. This is underlined by the fact that in Sijistān, east of Kirman, partisans of Qaṭarī, encouraged by his emissaries, gained control and minted coins in his name in the capital Zarang in 75/694–695.[16] Qaṭarī had played a leading part in the Muslim conquest of Sijistān under ʿAbd al-Raḥmān b. Samura and, according to the *Tārīkh-i Sīstān,* had gained many friends among the people of the province.[17] Still much later the Khārijites of Sijistān

12. See G. C. Miles, "Some Arab-Sassanian and Related Coins," p. 203; idem, "Some New Light on the History of Kirmān in the First Century of the Hijrah," p. 92.

13. The conflict between Nāfiʿ b. al-Azraq and Najda b. ʿĀmir is described by al-Mubarrad (*al-Kāmil,* p. 611) and al-Shahrastānī (p. 93) as revolving around the question whether *taqiyya,* precautionary concealment of beliefs, was licit or not.

14. Wellhausen, *Oppositionsparteien,* p. 35, n. 3. In the years immediately preceding the arrival of ʿAṭiyya it was evidently under the control of Muṣʿab b. al-Zubayr in whose name coins were struck there in the years 69, 70?, 71, and 72?. See J. Walker, *A Catalogue of the Arab-Sassanian Coins,* p. cxxi.

15. Walker, pp. lx, cxxi; Miles, "Some New Light," p. 90.

16. Walker, pp. lxi, cxxxi.

17. *Tārīkh-i Sīstān,* ed. M. Bahār, pp. 109–110.

seem to have been particularly attached to his memory.[18] The schism between them and the Khārijites of Kirman in the ʿAbbasid age may thus be partly rooted in the earlier rivalry between Qaṭarī and ʿAṭiyya, though this cannot be documented.

The final defeat of the Khārijites by al-Muhallab b. Abī Ṣufra was facilitated by a split of Qaṭarī's army. According to the account of al-Mubarrad, 8,000 men, mostly *mawālī* joined by a few Arabs, deserted him in protest against some decision and chose the *mawlā* ʿAbd Rabbih al-Ṣaghīr as their leader. While they, after some fighting, withdrew to Jīruft in Kirman, Qaṭarī, with a smaller Arab following, left for Ray.[19] Al-Muhallab now, probably in 76/695, attacked and killed ʿAbd Rabbih. ʿAṭiyya was forced to leave for Sijistān and Sind and was eventually, between 78 and 82, killed in Qandabīl.[20] Qaṭarī was tracked down and killed in Ṭabaristān in 78/697 or 79/698.

During the next decades Khārijism in Iran was reorganized by ʿAbd al-Karīm b. ʿAjarrad. Very little is known about him and his activity. According to some he was from Balkh, but this may have been merely a local rumor.[21] He was put in prison by Khālid al-Qasrī, governor of Iraq and Khurasan (106–120/724–738), and died there. Most heresiographers describe him as a follower of ʿAṭiyya b. al-Aswad or as belonging to the ʿAṭawiyya.[22] The revolutionary fervor of the Azāriqa had spent itself for a time and the more moderate attitudes of the ʿAṭawiyya were evidently better suited for what was viewed by the Khārijites as a period of *taqiyya*, a non-revolutionary phase of caution. Less credible is a report that Ibn ʿAjarrad had been a companion of Abū Bayhas, a Khārijite leader associated with religious debates in

18. *Tārīkh-i Sīstān*, pp. 131, 156.

19. Al-Mubarrad, p. 686. Other accounts differ concerning details including the numbers involved. According to Abū Mikhnaf, the *mawālī* were led by ʿAbd Rabbih al-Kabīr and Qaṭarī was left with only a fourth or fifth of his followers (al-Ṭabarī, II, p. 1006). The account of ʿAbd al-Qāhir al-Baghdādī (*al-Farq*, pp. 65–66) speaks of three groups: 7,000 following ʿAbd Rabbih al-Kabīr, 4,000 joining ʿAbd Rabbih al-Ṣaghīr, and above 10,000 staying with Qaṭarī. Al-Yaʿqūbī (II, p. 329) also mentions these three groups and states that Qaṭarī left for Ṭabaristān with 22,000 men.

20. Al-Balādhurī, *Ansāb al-ashrāf*, in W. Ahlwardt, *Anonyme arabische Chronik*, p. 135.

21. See Nashwān al-Ḥimyarī, *al-Ḥūr al-ʿīn*, p. 171. The report goes back to Abu l-Qāsim al-Balkhī who added that according to others it rather was Ibn ʿAjarrad's follower Maymūn who came from Balkh. In al-Ashʿarī's report (*maqālāt*, p. 9 1.9–10), which is evidently based on al-Balkhī's, *wa-Maymūn* should perhaps be read *aw Maymūn*.

22. This is expressly stated by al-Baghdādī, *al-Farq*, p. 72. Only pseudo-Nāshiʾ (*Masāʾil*, p. 69) describes the Khāzimiyya, which name he applies to the ʿAjārida in Sijistān, as the remnants of the Azāriqa after their military defeat. This may be a reflection of the sentimental attachment of the Khārijites of Sijistān to the Azraqī leader Qaṭarī.

Arabia and Iraq.[23] Ibn ʿAjarrad rather was active in Iran. In contrast to the other Khārijite movements of the time, the ʿAjārida, his followers, were not centered in Iraq. All the numerous later subsects of the ʿAjārida mentioned by the heresiographers were located in various regions of eastern Iran. There is no evidence for any presence of them elsewhere. Ibn ʿAjarrad may thus be considered the founder of a Persian Khārijism at least in a geographical sense.

The first schism among the ʿAjārida occurred still before the imprisonment of Ibn ʿAjarrad as a result of a doctrinal dispute with one of his companions, Thaʿlaba b. Mushkān, probably a Persian *mawlā*.[24] Ibn ʿAjarrad took the position that minor children were not subject to either *walāya* or *barāʾa* until they reach maturity and are invited to affirm Islam,[25] while Thaʿlaba, whose own daughter's status was involved in the dispute, held that the religious status of minors followed that of their parents. His daughter was thus a Muslim in his view and as such entitled to *walāya* whereas the children of religious opponents deserved *barāʾa*.[26] Ibn ʿAjarrad and Thaʿlaba now dissociated from

23. Al-Ashʿarī, *maqālāt,* p. 95; al-Shahrastānī, p. 95. That Ibn ʿAjarrad left Abū Bayhas over the question of the legitimacy of selling a slave woman to non-Khārijites, as the report of al-Ashʿarī states, is quite unlikely. There is no evidence that Ibn ʿAjarrad agreed with any of the particular views of Abū Bayhas mentioned by the heresiographers. The discussion about the sale of slave women seems to have taken place in Arabia. Ibrāhīm, whose proposed sale of a slave girl provoked the controversy, was a Medinan (Nashwān, p. 175), and Abū Bayhas is known to have sought refuge in Medina from the persecution of al-Ḥajjāj. According to al-Baghdādī Abū Bayhas was at first a follower of Abū Fudayk, the dissident Najdī leader in Arabia (*al-Farq,* p. 69). Al-Ḥakam b. Marwān, the founder of a subdivision of the Bayhasiyya called Aṣḥāb al-suʾāl, was a Kufan (al-Ashʿarī, p. 112). In a doctrinal statement ascribed to Abū Bayhas it is assumed that the imam is in Kufa (al-Malaṭī, *al-Tanbīh wa l-radd,* p. 137).

24. His father's name is given by al-Baghdādī (*al-Farq,* p. 80) as Mushkān. In the other accounts it is given as ʿĀmir. The father was evidently given an Arabic name when he became a Muslim or in order to hide his non-Arab origin, as was common practice. On the same basis Ḥamza b. Ādharak, the Khārijite leader, is regularly called Ḥamza b. ʿAbd Allāh in the *Tārīkh-i Sīstān.*

25. The heresiographers mostly assert that according to Ibn ʿAjarrad all children were subject to *barāʾa* until they reached majority and were invited to affirm Islam. This is most likely a hostile distortion of his doctrine. He can hardly have asked his followers to dissociate from their minor children. Abu l-Qāsim al-Balkhī lists a separate, anonymous group of ʿAjārida who held that the children of believers and unbelievers were not subject to either *walāya* or enmity (*ʿadāwa* = *barāʾa*) until they reached maturity and affirmed Islam (Nashwān, p. 172).

26. Al-Ashʿarī at first (p. 97, ll. 7–9) erroneously attributes the doctrine of the ʿAjārida to the Thaʿāliba by conflating Abu l-Qāsim al-Balkhī's last, anonymous group of the ʿAjārida, whose doctrine was quoted above in note 25, with his first group of the Thaʿāliba. Later (p. 100, ll. 14–15) he gives the correct view of the Thaʿāliba also quoting al-Balkhī (see Nashwān, p. 172). Al-Ashʿarī's error has also crept into the account of al-Shahrastānī (p. 98, ll. 3–5).

each other as infidels. According to ʿAbd al-Qāhir al-Baghdādī, the Thaʿāliba, Thaʿlaba's followers, continued to consider Ibn ʿAjarrad as their imam before the dispute and held that Thaʿlaba then became the imam.[27] The Thaʿāliba and their subsects prevailed in northeastern Iran while the ʿAjārida in the south remained loyal to their leader.

Thaʿlaba must have died some time before the fall of the Umayyad caliphate. According to al-Baghdādī, the main body of the Thaʿāliba did not recognize an imam after him.[28] Their authority in religious matters was a certain Abū Khālid Ziyād b. ʿAbd al-Raḥmān al-Shaybānī, probably also a *mawlā*.[29] In 129/746–747 the Thaʿāliba became involved in the revolutionary turmoil of Khurasan. One of them, Shaybān b. Salama, an Arab of the Banū Sadūs, rose in revolt and quickly gathered a strong Khārijite army, said to have numbered 30,000 men, around himself. Many of his followers were Basran Khārijites. He brought Sarakhs, Ṭūs, and the area of Nishapur (Abr Shahr) under his control. When he joined forces with another rebel leader, Ibn al-Kirmānī, many Khārijites accused him of worldly ambition and deserted him. Ziyād b. ʿAbd al-Raḥmān, chief of the Thaʿāliba, "stayed in his house."[30] The turbulent conditions further forced Shaybān to enter briefly into changing alliances with Abū Muslim al-Khurāsānī, the leader of the ʿAbbasid revolutionary movement, and Naṣr b. Sayyār, the Umayyad governor, before being attacked and killed by the army of the former in Shaʿbān 130/April 748.[31] His supporters among the Thaʿāliba, known as the Shaybāniyya, continued to hold him in esteem asserting that he had repented of his offenses before his death. They were led by ʿAṭiyya al-Jūzjānī and lived dispersed, mostly in the regions of Jūzjān, Nasā, and Abīward.[32] Their opponents, the Ziyādiyya, argued that his offenses in siding with Abū Muslim involved the killing of Muslims and seizing their property and that

27. *Al-Farq,* p. 80.

28. *Al-Farq,* p. 80.

29. Thus his name is given by al-Shahrastānī (p. 99). He is presumably identical with the Khārijite chief ʿAbd al-Raḥmān b. Ziyād, *mawlā* of Quraysh, who is mentioned by Khalīfa b. Khayyāṭ (*Taʾrīkh,* p. 388) as opposing Shaybān b. Salama. See below n. 30.

30. Khalīfa, *Taʾrikh,* p. 388: *qaʿada ʿAbd al-Raḥmān b. Ziyād mawlā li-Quraysh fī baytih wa-kāna raʾsan fīhim.* This puts him as a local leader in contrast to the leaders of the Basran Khārijites mentioned previously in Khalīfa's account.

31. The most detailed account of Shaybān's relations with Abū Muslim and Naṣr b. Sayyār is provided by the *Akhbār al-dawla al-ʿAbbāsiyya,* ed. ʿA. al-Dūrī and ʿA. al-Muṭṭalibī, pp. 281–322. See also al-Ṭabarī, II, pp. 1989–1997; Khalīfa, pp. 388–390.

32. Al-Baghdādī, *al-Milal wa l-niḥal,* ed. A. N. Nader, p. 74; *Tūrkhān* read *Jūzjān.* In al-Shahrastānī's account (p. 99) these place-names appear, evidently corrupted, as Jurjān, Nasā and Armenia (Armaniyya), and that of their leader as ʿAṭiyya al-Jurjānī.

repentance in such circumstances was not acceptable without retaliation and restitution or forgiveness on the part of the next-of-kin. They thus dissociated from Shaybān and his supporters.

The scanty notes which the heresiographers provide concerning the other splinter sects of the Thaʿāliba indicate that they were able to organize in autonomous communities and to gather and distribute the alms tax among themselves. The Akhnasiyya, followers of al-Akhnas b. Qays, greatly toned down the common Khārijite militancy thus easing their relations with other Muslims. They abstained from dissociating from, or associating with, any Muslim except those whose faith or infidelity was definitely known. They forbade clandestine murder of any Muslim and theft of their property and held that no Muslim must be fought before having been summoned to the (Khārijite) faith unless they specifically knew his being opposed to their beliefs. They also permitted marrying their women to grave sinners who, in the common Khārijite view, were polytheists.

On this latter point al-Akhnas was specifically opposed by Maʿbad b. ʿAbd al-Raḥmān, leader of the Maʿbadiyya. Maʿbad also opposed the rule introduced by Thaʿlaba that slaves should pay alms taxes (*zakawāt*) if they had the means (*idha staghnaw*) and should be given of them if they were poor. This rule evidently envisages a higher degree of the right of slaves to property than is usually granted by Islamic law. According to one report, the upholders of this doctrine among the Thaʿāliba further ruled that the master does not inherit from his slave.[33] Maʿbad apparently inclined to a more conventional view. He did not, however, dissociate from Thaʿlaba because of this disagreement.[34]

The Thaʿāliba at first also deviated from the common rule of Islamic law in paying only half the tithe (*ʿushr*) on land watered directly from streams and canals. Ziyād b. ʿAbd al-Raḥmān then informed them that they must pay the full tithe but forbade dissociation from those who held that only the half-tithe was due. A certain Rushayd al-Ṭūsī argued that if paying only the half-tithe was not subject to dissociation they should continue to pay no more. His followers, known as the Rushaydiyya or ʿUshriyya, lived presumably in the region of Ṭūs.

The last sect of the Thaʿāliba mentioned by the heresiographers,

33. Khushaysh in al-Malaṭī, p. 136.

34. Al-Shahrastānī, p. 98. His account of the sects of the Thaʿāliba seems generally better informed than that of the other heresiographers, who rather ascribe the rule to Maʿbad.

called the Mukramiyya, deviated on purely theological grounds. Their leader Mukram b. ᶜAbd Allāh al-ᶜIjlī[35] taught that anyone failing to perform the ritual prayer or committing another major sin was an infidel, not because of his act, but because he was ignorant of God. This "ignorance" (*jahl*) could, however, be a willful ignoring and disregarding of God's commandments. He argued that anybody having a true knowledge of God, of His cognizance of man's hidden motives, and of His reward and punishment could commit such sins only in wanton disregard of it. The doctrine reflects a heightened meaning of "knowledge of God" as faith and fear of Him (*taqwā*) similar to the teaching of al-Ḥasan al-Baṣrī who identified faith with overpowering fear of God which would not allow the faithful to disobey His commandments. It was in conflict with the common view of the Khārijites and the Muᶜtazila who defined faith as comprising two distinct aspects, intellectual knowledge of God and acts in accordance with His Commandments. The Mukramiyya also upheld the doctrine of *muwāfāt,* i.e., that God's friendship (*muwālāt*) and enmity (*muᶜādāt*) toward men did not depend on their acts throughout their lives but on their final state as believers or unbelievers before their death. The doctrine was mostly opposed by the Muᶜtazila as implying predestination but later became widespread among the Sunnites, especially the Ashᶜarites, and to some extent among Twelver Shiᶜites.[36]

The followers of Ibn ᶜAjarrad in Sijistān became active soon after Khālid al-Qasrī succeeded to the governorship of Iraq and the east in 106/724.[37] The imprisonment of Ibn ᶜAjarrad by Khālid may well have been connected with the suppression of this rebellion. During the upheavals preceding the overthrow of the Umayyad caliphate the Khārijites of Sijistān and southern Iran evidently lacked an ambitious leader and were only on a minor scale involved in fighting. For a brief time some of them backed Shaybān b. ᶜAbd al-ᶜAzīz al-Yashkurī, a Ṣufrī Khārijite leader who had been driven out of northern Mesopotamia by the Umayyad army. They occupied Zarang, the capital of Sijistān, and successfully resisted ᶜAbd Allāh b. Muᶜāwiya, another revolutionary leader backed primarily by Shiᶜites. Shaybān al-Yashkurī soon left, however, and was later killed in ᶜOman.[38]

While Ibn ᶜAjarrad was still alive in prison, a theological dispute

35. See al-Shahrastānī, p. 99. In all other sources the leader is called simply Abū Mukram.
36. See E. Kohlberg, "Muwāfāt Doctrines in Muslim Theology."
37. See Bosworth, *Sīstān,* p. 73.
38. Bosworth, *Sīstān,* pp. 76–77.

arose among his followers. A certain Maymūn b. Khālid adopted the doctrine of human free will associated with the Qadariyya and the Muᶜtazila while his opponent, Shuᶜayb b. Muḥammad, upheld divine determinism. Ibn ᶜAjarrad was asked by letter to settle the dispute. His answer suggested a compromise: "We say that whatever God wills happens and whatever He wills not does not happen. Yet we do not fix evil upon God." Both Maymūn and Shuᶜayb claimed to be vindicated and held on to their conflicting views.[39]

The heresiographers speak of two sects, the Maymūniyya and the Shuᶜaybiyya, arising out of this quarrel. It does not seem, however, that the disagreement was serious enough to bring about an effective split at this stage. During the early ᶜAbbasid age the ᶜAjārida were generally called the Khāzimiyya, after a leader, Khāzim b. ᶜAlī, about whom nothing else is known. The earliest heresiographical source, pseudo-Nāshiʾ, apparently knows the ᶜAjārida only under that name.[40] ᶜAbd al-Qāhir al-Baghdādī describes the Khāzimiyya as "most of the ᶜAjārida of Sijistān."[41] The same people are presumably also meant in al-Malaṭī's account of a Khārijite group whom he calls simply al-Ḥarūriyya, a general name for the Khārijites, and of whom he says: "They are in the region of Sijistān, Herat, and Khurasan. They are a numerous people, only God knows their number. They possess horses and bravery. Their women fight on slender horses just like their men fight."[42] Abu l-Qāsim al-Balkhī, on the other hand, asserts that the Maymūniyya and the ᶜAjārida were predominant in Khurasan and Sijistān.[43] These global statements suggest that there were initially no sharp sectarian divisions among the former followers of Ibn ᶜAjarrad.

The heresiographers offer various details about the deviant beliefs and practices of the Khāzimiyya whose reliability is difficult to judge. Of particular interest is the early account of pseudo-Nāshiʾ which differs considerably from the later reports.[44] According to him, the Khāzimiyya forbade the pilgrimage to Mekka during the time of *taqiyya.* Only when they would be able to carry out their religious duty

39. Al-Ashᶜarī, pp. 94–95.

40. *Masāʾil,* p. 69. As noted (above n. 22) the Khāzimiyya are treated in this account as a branch of the Azāriqa. Only the beginning of pseudo-Nāshiʾ's account of the Najadāt is extant (p. 70). It does not seem likely, however, that he would have derived any of the other sects of the ᶜAjārida from them.

41. *Al-Farq,* p. 73.

42. Al-Malaṭī, p. 42. In the original text, the last sentence precedes the rest.

43. Nashwān, p. 171. Al-Balkhī apparently did not mention the Shuᶜaybiyya at all.

44. *Masāʾil,* p. 69. The independence and archaic character of pseudo-Nāshiʾ's account of the Khārijites supports the other indications that the work was composed well before the time of al-Nāshiʾ al-Akbar.

of "ordering and prohibiting," when *taqiyya* would cease and its abode would become an abode of Islam, the duty of the pilgrimage would become obligatory. In the meantime people were obliged to cooperate in righteousness and fear of God without concealing the clear proofs and guidance revealed by God. The measure was evidently motivated by the desire to avoid friction with other Muslims during the pilgrimage.

The Khāzimiyya further rejected the punishment of stoning (for adultery) and permitted marriage of a second wife together with her paternal or maternal aunt. The latter detail stands in contrast to the later report of the Sunnite theologian al-Ḥusayn al-Karābīsī (d. 248/862) that "the ʿAjārida and the Maymūniyya," obviously meaning pseudo-Nāshiʾ's Khāzimiyya, permitted the marriage of granddaughter and granddaughters of brothers and sisters,[45] a doctrine which ʿAbd al-Qāhir al-Baghdādī was quick to denounce as derived from the Zoroastrian religion.[46] In view of the more modest deviation reported by pseudo-Nāshiʾ, it may be suspected that al-Karābīsī's report merely represents a polemical deduction from the opponents' premises which was a popular practice among rival theologians. According to pseudo-Nāshiʾ, the Khāzimiyya based their abnormal doctrines on the principle that only religious laws stipulated by the Qurʾan or unanimously agreed by all Muslims were binding. Qurʾan IV 23 forbade Muslims to marry the mother of their wives or their stepdaughter but not the aunts of their wives. By generalizing the principle to other parts of the Qurʾanic verse permission to marry one's granddaughters could readily be deduced.[47]

Quite insignificant, if not a heresiographical creation, was evidently a "sect" which according to pseudo-Nāshiʾ separated from the Khāzimiyya and is called by him simply "the Innovators" (Bidaʿiyya). They held on the basis of Qurʾan XI 114 that there were only two obligatory ritual prayers, one during daytime and one at night. They are also

45. Al-Ashʿarī, p. 95. The other sources, all ultimately dependent on al-Karābīsī, are evidently mistaken in confining the doctrine to the Maymūniyya in particular.

46. *Al-Farq,* p. 264. Al-Baghdādī's view has been accepted by some modern scholars. See, for instance, Watt, *The Formative Period,* p. 34. Watt further suggests that Maymūn's words in connection with his doctrine of human free will, "We do not fix evil upon God," might link up with the Zoroastrian dualism of good and evil. The desire not to attribute evil to God was, however, expressed by the Qadariyya in general, including al-Ḥasan al-Baṣrī. There is no good reason to assume that in the case of Maymūn it derived from Zoroastrianism. The sentence "We do not fix evil upon God" is, moreover, attributed by al-Ashʿarī (p. 95) to Ibn ʿAjarrad rather than to Maymūn.

47. All the reports imply that the doctrine ascribed by al-Karābīsī to the ʿAjārida and Maymūniyya was based on Qurʾan IV 23.

said to have required the ritual slaughter of fish caught alive.[48] Poorly attested is a charge that the Maymūniyya excluded the sūra of Yūsuf from the Qurʾan.[49] Al-Shahrastānī quotes an anonymous report about the Khāzimiyya according to which they refrained from judgment concerning the conduct of ʿAlī and did not explicitly dissociate from him.[50] The reliability of this information must be viewed with caution since any positive view of ʿAlī would have been inconsistent with the basis of Khārijism.

There are also reports about theological disputes among the Khāzimiyya. The Maʿlūmiyya among them were said to have maintained that whoever does not know God by all His names is ignorant of Him, while the Majhūliyya held that it was sufficient to know God by some of His names. The descriptive names Maʿlūmiyya and Majhūliyya suggest that these were schools of thought turned into separate sects by the heresiographers. The Maʿlūmiyya further upheld two apparently conflicting positions. Like the Qadariyya, they denied that human acts are created by God and, like the predestinarians, they taught that the capacity (*istiṭāʿa*) to act was simultaneous with the act and that everything happened according to the will of God. The doctrine is probably based on the compromise reply of Ibn ʿAjarrad to Maymūn and Shuʿayb and indicates that the controversy about free will versus predestination continued to be alive among the Khāzimiyya although it hardly was so productive of sectarian schisms as the heresiographers suggest.

The genuine schisms were rather caused by conflicts about the leadership. Among the Khārijites of Kirman and Makrān a leader called Khalaf rose around the year 179/795. According to the *Tārīkh-i Sīstān,* some 5,000 Khārijites of Sijistān assembled to back him but Ḥamza b. Ādharak persuaded them to swear allegiance to himself.[51] This produced the permanent schism of the Khārijites of Kirman and Makrān who were henceforth known as the Khalafiyya. The heresiographers rather stress that they were predestinarians and at odds with the Maymūniyya upholding human free will. But this disagreement

48. *Masāʾil,* pp. 69–70.

49. Al-Ashʿarī (p. 96) presents it as a report which he was unable to verify. Al-Baghdādī ascribes the report to al-Karābīsī (*al-Farq,* p. 265). This seems to be based on a faulty reading of *ḥukiya lanā* in al-Ashʿarī's text as *ḥakā lanā.* Al-Karābīsī was the subject in al-Ashʿarī's previous report. According to al-Shahrastānī (p. 96) both al-Balkhī and al-Ashʿarī quoted the report. It is missing, however, in Nashwān al-Ḥimyarī's account based on al-Balkhī (*al-Ḥūr,* p. 171).

50. Al-Shahrastānī, p. 97.

51. *Tārīkh-i Sīstān,* p. 156.

was clearly not the basis of the schism. Khalaf was later apparently succeeded as imam of the Khalafiyya by Masʿūd b. Qays who was attacked by Ḥamza and drowned during his flight in a river valley. His followers had doubts about his death and were hoping for his return.[52] According to Abu l-Qāsim al-Balkhī, they affirmed that it would not be licit for them to pledge allegiance to an imam until 120 years passed from his birthday.[53] In the meantime they evidently considered themselves in a time of *taqiyya* and abstained from revolutionary activity.[54] There is no further mention of the Khalafiyya.

Ḥamza b. Ādharak, the most famous of the eastern Khārijite leaders, was a descendant of a Persian *dihqān* from Sijistān. He became a follower of the Khārijite rebel al-Ḥuḍayn of Ūq, a *mawlā* who rose in Sijistān in 175/791–792 and was killed in 177/793.[55] Then he killed a tax official who would not accept his warnings to act in accordance with the religious law and was forced to leave Sijistān. After his return he gained the allegiance of the Khārijite rebels who had assembled in support of Khalaf. At first he probably did not wish to repudiate the leadership of the latter. This early attitude is most likely reflected in the doctrine attributed to him that there might be more than one legitimate imam at a time when the Khārijites were not united and the enemies were not yet subdued.[56]

Later, however, Ḥamza came into conflict with the other Khārijite communities in the region. According to al-Baghdādī, he attacked the Bayhasiyya killing many of them. This is the only mention of that branch of Khārijism in the east. It was presumably a small group of converts from the ʿAjārida. At that time Ḥamza adopted the title of Commander of the Faithful,[57] thus apparently announcing his claim to universal leadership. Next he sent a raiding party against the Khāzimiyya in the region of Faljird (Fargird), west of Būshanj (Pūshang) in Qūhistān, and they committed a great massacre among their coreligionists.[58] Ḥamza's attack on the Khalafiyya in Kirman has already

52. *Al-Farq,* p. 78.
53. Nashwān, p. 171.
54. *Al-Farq,* p. 75. Al-Baghdādī is mistaken in explaining their quietism by a lack of someone suitable for the imamate. B. Składanek asserts, without offering any evidence, that the Khārijite movement in Kirman and Makrān "clearly did not accept Iranian elements" ("The Khārijites in Iran," I, p. 88). This is thoroughly unlikely.
55. See Bosworth, *Sīstān,* p. 92. As Bosworth points out, al-Shahrastānī's statement that Ḥamza was a follower of al-Ḥuḍayn b. Ruqād seems to rest on a confusion with an earlier Khārijite rebel of that name who was killed in 140/757–758.
56. Al-Balkhī in Nashwān, p. 171; al-Shahrastānī, p. 96.
57. *Al-Farq,* p. 77.
58. *Al-Farq,* p. 78; Bosworth, *Sīstān,* p. 93.

been mentioned. Immediately afterwards he carried out a murderous campaign against the Thaʿāliba in the district (*rustāq*) of Busht (Pūsht) southwest of Nishapur.[59]

The heresiographers view the Ḥamziyya primarily as opposed to the Khāzimiyya in the question of human free will versus predestination. While the Khāzimiyya affirmed determinism and the doctrine of *muwāfāt,* like the Mukramiyya, holding that friendship and enmity belonged to the attributes of God's essence and thus were eternal and unchangeable, the Ḥamziyya, like the Maymūniyya, upheld human free will. In conflict with the concept of divine justice usually implied in the latter doctrine, they are said, however, to have affirmed that the minor children of the "polytheists," i.e., their Muslim opponents, were condemned to hell, although they did not deserve it for any of their actions. According to al-Shahrastānī, the Khalafiyya in particular criticized them for this inconsistency.[60] The attitude of the Ḥamziyya in this question, if it is correctly reported,[61] may have been influenced more by considerations concerning the practical conduct of war than by theoretical speculation. They probably killed children of their enemies together with their parents.

Other heresiographical reports about the Ḥamziyya deal specifically with aspects of the conduct of war and relations with other Muslims. The Ḥamziyya held that only the government and its supporters and critics of their own religious teaching should be fought.[62] This gave Ḥamza and other leaders of the Ḥamziyya some room for action in forming alliances with other antigovernment forces. In peacetime the followers of Ḥamza held the killing of any Muslim and clandestine seizure of property to be illicit.[63] Even in wartime, according to al-Malaṭī, they did not allow taking anything as booty unless the owner had been killed.[64] A distorting exaggeration is probably al-Baghdādī's

59. *Al-Farq,* p. 79: *Bust* read *Busht.* On the region see Yāqūt, *Muʿjam,* s.v. Busht, and G. Le Strange, *The Lands of the Eastern Caliphate,* p. 354.

60. Al-Shahrastānī, p. 97.

61. The earlier heresiographers, al-Balkhī and al-Ashʿarī, do not mention it.

62. Al-Ashʿarī, p. 94. Al-Balkhī (Nashwān, p. 171) and al-Shahrastānī (p. 96) attribute this doctrine already to the Maymūniyya.

63. Al-Ashʿarī, p. 94, quoting Zurqān.

64. Al-Malaṭī, pp. 42–43. Opposed to this doctrine were, according to al-Malaṭī (p. 43), the Ṣalīdiyya, who also belonged to the Ḥamziyya but held killing and seizure of the enemies' property to be licit under all conditions. They were the most vicious of the Khārijites and there were many of them in the region of Sijistān. The Ṣalīdiyya may be identical with the Ṣaltiyya, followers of ʿUthmān b. Abi l-Ṣalt and al-Ṣalt b. Abi l-Ṣalt, mentioned by the other heresiographers. They are said to have associated with those who converted to their religious doctrine but to have dissociated from the minor children of the converts until they reached maturity and accepted their doctrine.

assertion that Ḥamza considered all booty illicit and would order to burn the property of defeated enemies, to hamstring their riding animals, and to kill the captives.[65]

After the death of the caliph Hārūn al-Rashīd in 193/809 relieved Ḥamza of the danger of a major ʿAbbasid offensive, he moved out of Sijistān to Ghūr and India. Few details are known about his activities there, but his aim was evidently to spread his Khārijite Islam in non-Muslim territory. According to the *Tārīkh-i Sīstān,* he (re)founded the town of Gardīz east of Ghazna. The inhabitants of the town were still described as Khārijites in the *Ḥudūd al-ʿālam* written about 372/983. It seems that it was ruled by a line of Khārijite amīrs until it was conquered by the Ṣaffārids after 364/974.[66]

Missionary activity of the followers of Ḥamza in the territories outside the Muslim world is reflected in al-Shahrastānī's report about a branch of the Ḥamziyya called the Aṭrāfiyya. They held that the people in the outlying regions (*aṣḥāb al-aṭrāf*) were excused from performing the duties of the religious law which they ignored. Their aim was no doubt to facilitate the conversion of non-Muslims without immediately imposing upon them all the intricacies of the ritual and legal obligations of the *sharīʿa.* In this respect they adopted the position of the Murjiʾa. Like the Muʿtazila, however, they affirmed that there were rational obligations, presumably recognition of the unity of God and the mission of Muḥammad and other prophets, which the "people of the outlying regions" must fulfill. The chief of the Aṭrāfiyya was a man from Sijistān, Ghālib b. Shādhil, and they were opposed by one ʿAbd Allāh al-Sadīwarī(?).[67]

Ḥamza remained the leader of the Khārijites of Sijistān for more than three decades until his death in 213/828. His career and military exploits made a great impression on the popular mind in eastern Iran which is reflected in the admiration expressed for him in the *Tārīkh-i Sīstān.* The author refers to a *Story of the Campaigns of Ḥamza (Qiṣṣa-*

65. Al-Baghdādī, *al-Milal,* p. 711; *al-Farq,* p. 77.

66. See A. D. H. Bivar, art. "Gardīz" in *E.I.,* 2nd ed. The possibility of Khārijite activity in the Tochi valley of Wazīristān in the third/ninth century has been suggested by Bosworth ("Notes on the Pre-Ghaznawid History of Eastern Afghanistan," pp. 22–24; *Sīstān,* p. 104).

67. Al-Shahrastānī, pp. 96–97, where the last name appears as al-S-rnūrī. The reading al-Sadīwarī is given in the edition of al-Shahrastānī by ʿAbd al-Laṭīf Muḥ. al-ʿĪr, Cairo 1977, p. 133. Sadīwar was a town in the region of Marw (al-Samʿanī, *al-Ansāb,* s.v. al-Sadīwarī; Yāqūt, s.v. Sadīwar). The approximate time of the rise of the Aṭrāfiyya is indicated by al-Shahrastānī's further statement that the Muḥammadiyya, who belonged to them, were led by a former follower of al-Ḥuḍayn (of Ūq), Muḥammad b. Rizq(?).

yi maghāzī-yi Ḥamza) which described the legendary expeditions of Ḥamza to India, Ceylon, China, Turkestan, and Anatolia. This story, it has been suggested, influenced the popular romance of the amīr Ḥamza b. ʿAbd al-Muṭṭalib, the uncle of the Prophet, widespread in Persian, Arabic and Turkish.[68]

After Ḥamza's death his followers swore allegiance to Abū Isḥāq Ibrāhīm b. ʿUmayr, a learned man from Jāshan (Gāshan) in Sijistān as their Commander of the Faithful. He soon proved too conciliatory for them, forbidding them to plunder their Sunnite opponents, and was forced to flee and go into hiding. The Khārijites now, in 215/830, chose Abū ʿAwf b. ʿAbd al-Raḥmān b. Bazīʿ, who came from the town of Kurink north of Zarang.[69] He carried on the war against the government and against the infidels in the east. The date of his death is unknown. He was succeeded by ʿAmmār b. Yāsir al-Khārijī who revolted in the region of Kish in Sijistān in 238/853 and also seems to have claimed the title of Commander of the Faithful.[70] The fortunes of the Khārijites in Sijistān were reversed now with the rise of Yaʿqūb b. al-Layth al-Ṣaffār. ʿAmmār was defeated and killed in battle by him in 251/865. Around 258/872 the Khārijites revolted at Karūkh, east of Herat, under a certain ʿAbd al-Raḥīm or ʿAbd al-Raḥmān who adopted the title of Commander of the Faithful and the caliphal name al-Mutawakkil ʿala llāh. They took possession of the region around Herat and Isfizār. Yaʿqūb attacked them and forced ʿAbd al-Raḥīm into submission appointing him as his governor of Isfizār. Within a year the Khārijites killed him and paid homage to Ibrāhīm b. al-Akhḍar in his stead. He, too, quickly submitted to Yaʿqūb and was appointed by him as commander of the "army of Khārijites" *(jaysh al-shurāt)*.[71] Many Khārijites had previously been enlisted in Yaʿqūb's army.[72] Others, who resisted, including a group in Bamm in eastern Kirman, were wiped out.[73]

The military strength of the Khārijites in eastern Iran was permanently broken. Khārijite communities are, however, still mentioned throughout the fourth/tenth century. In Bamm in Kirman they held one of the three congregational mosques in town where they kept

68. See Bahār, introd. to the edition of *Tārīkh-i Sīstān,* p. *Lām Gīm;* idem, *Sabk-shināsī,* I, pp. 283–285; G. Meredith-Owens, art. "Ḥamza b. ʿAbd al-Muṭṭalib" in *E.I.,* 2nd ed.
69. Ibn Rusta, *al-Aʿlāq al-Nafīsa,* p. 174; Bosworth, *Sīstān,* p. 104, n. 5.
70. See *Tārīkh-i Sīstān,* p. 203, where Yaʿqūb b. al-Layth is quoted as warning him against this claim.
71. *Tārīkh-i Sīstān,* pp. 207, 217–218.
72. Bosworth, "The Armies of the Ṣaffārids," pp. 541–544, 549.
73. *Tārīkh-i Sīstān,* p. 213.

their own treasury (*bayt māl*). They were few but wealthy, probably engaged in trade.[74] Makrān is described by al-Masʿūdī as "the land of the Khārijites (*arḍ al-Khawārij*)."[75] In the region around Zarang in Sijistān, the towns of Juwayn (Guwayn), Karkūya, Zanbūq, and Kurink (Kurūn) were solidly Khārijite, while Farah was half Khārijite and half Sunnite.[76] According to Yāqūt, the Khārijites of Karkūya practiced "fasting, prayer, and excessive worship and had their own jurists and scholars."[77] Further north toward Herat, Isfizār (Aspuzār), comprising four towns, was partly inhabited by Khārijites.[78] In the region of Herat, there were many Khārijites in the towns of Karūkh and Astarabyān.[79] Further east, besides Gardīz, the town of Alabān, located at a two-days' trip from Ghazna toward Kābul, was solidly Khārijite. The inhabitants claimed to be descendants of the Azāriqa pursued by al-Muhallab, but were now submissive to the government. Among them there were merchants, wealthy men, scholars, and men of letters. They had relations, presumably commercial, with the princes of India and Sind, and each one of their chiefs had both an Arabic and an Indian name.[80] The Khārijites of Sijistān were in this period generally known as most reliable partners in trade.[81] Others worked as weavers.[82] In the course of the fifth/eleventh century they seem to have been absorbed by Sunnism.

The Khārijism which al-Masʿūdī noted in Adharbayjan in the fourth/tenth century[83] was of a different kind. It was introduced there at various times from northern Mesopotamia (al-Jazīra) and the region of Mosul where it was rampant among the Arab tribe of Shaybān of Bakr ever since the Second Civil War. The Khārijite rebel Shabīb al-Shaybānī entered Adharbayjan briefly in 76/695–696.[84] Toward the

74. Al-Iṣṭakhrī, *al-Masālik,* pp. 167–168; Ibn Ḥawqal, *Ṣūrat al-arḍ,* p. 312; al-Maqdisī, p. 469.

75. Al-Masʿūdī, *Murūj al-dhahab,* § 251; also §§ 1994, 2190.

76. Al-Maqdisī, p. 305, who mentions a further Khārijite town whose reading is uncertain; Yāqūt, III, p. 42, IV, p. 269.

77. Yāqūt, III, p. 42.

78. *Ḥudūd al-ʿālam,* p. 104; al-Iṣṭakhri, p. 267, mentions specifically the mountain valley of Kāshkān with prosperous villages as inhabited by Khārijites, while the towns of Isfizār were Sunnite.

79. Al-Iṣṭakhrī, p. 266; Ibn Ḥawqal, p. 439; al-Maqdisī, p. 323.

80. Yāqūt, I, p. 438, quoting Abu l-Fatḥ Naṣr al-Iskandarī (d. 560/1165). If the latter is the author of the report, this would seem to be the latest mention of Khārijites in the east. It is not unlikely, however, that Naṣr is quoting a somewhat earlier source.

81. Yāqūt, III, p. 42, quoting al-Iṣṭakhrī.

82. Yāqūt, IV, p. 269.

83. Al-Masʿūdī, *Murūj,* §§ 1994, 2190.

84. Al-Ṭabarī, II, pp. 896, 916.

end of the Umayyad caliphate, the Khārijite al-Ḍaḥḥāk b. Qays al-Shaybānī, in revolt against Marwān II, found support in Adharbayjan. One of his men stationed at Darband, Musāfir al-Qassāb, rose and was joined by Khārijites (*shurāt*) in Ardabīl, Bājarwān, Warthān, and Baylaqān. After the defeat and death of al-Ḍaḥḥāk in 128/746, Musāfir still held out and was overthrown and killed only under the ʿAbbasid caliph al-Saffāḥ.[85] The insurrection of the Khārijite Hārūn al-Wāziqī (267–283/880–896) in Northern Mesopotamia also had later repercussions in Adharbayjan. After Hārūn's death one of his companions, the Kurd Ibrāhīm b. Shādhlūya, found refuge there and married the daughter of a local Kurdish chief. Their son Daysam b. Ibrāhīm, like his father a Khārijite, rose in the military service of Yūsuf b. Abi l-Sāj to prominence.[86] After the fall of the Sājid dynasty, he became involved in the struggle for the rule of Adharbayjan and by 326/938 he held sway over the province, backed mainly by Kurdish troops. Later he also seized Armenia for a time. His reign was disputed by the Musāfirid al-Marzubān b. Muḥammad who eventually, in 344/955–956, gained definite control. Daysam was blinded and imprisoned by him and was killed after al-Marzubān's death in 346/957.[87]

The Khārijites of Northern Mesopotamia were Ṣufrīs, and Daysam and his Kurdish followers no doubt also adhered to that branch of Khārijism. The Ṣufriyya and the Ibāḍiyya were the two movements which emerged out of the *qaʿada* in Basra, those Khārijites who refused to be drawn into the armed rebellion of Nāfiʿ b. al-Azraq and Najda b. ʿĀmir during the Second Civil War. The Ṣufriyya, however, maintained a relatively militant attitude and stood close to the Najadāt in their basic principles. Like the Azāriqa and the Najadāt they considered the non-Khārijite Muslims and all grave sinners as infidels and polytheists and their territory as *dār kufr wa-shirk*.[88] According to al-Shahrastānī, Ziyād b. al-Aṣfar, the reputed founder of the Ṣufriyya, held that there were two kinds of polytheism, one consisting of obedience to the devil and the other of idol worship, and two kinds of infidelity, one by ingratitude (toward God, *kufr niʿma*) and the other denial of the Lordship.[89] Muslim offenders thus were infidels by in-

85. Al-Balādhurī, *Futūḥ al-buldān*, p. 209.
86. Ibn al-Athīr, VIII, p. 385. V. Minorsky suggested that Daysam's father was Arab and only his mother Kurdish (*Studies in Caucasian History*, pp. 113–114; *E.I.*, 2nd ed., art. "Kurd," section iii B). This does not seem to be implied in Ibn al-Athīr's report.
87. See *Cambridge History of Iran*, IV, pp. 232–235.
88. Al-Ashʿarī, pp. 118, 463.
89. Al-Shahrastānī, p. 102. Ziyād added that there were also two kinds of dissociation (*barāʾa*), dissociation from those committing sins liable to Qurʾanic punishments (*ḥudud*),

gratitude and polytheists by obeying the devil. Like the Najadāt, the Ṣufriyya did not permit the killing of women and children of their Muslim enemies and did not consider their children as infidels, even though their fathers were polytheists in their eyes. They distinguished between times of *taqiyya,* when dissemblance was permitted in words but not in acts, and times of open rebellion (*ʿalāniya*). Those of their community who abstained from fighting were not considered infidels.[90] The heresiographers do not report any particulars about the doctrine of Daysam and his followers. According to al-Masʿūdī, many of the Kurds of Adharbayjan, among them Ibn Shādhlūya, were Khārijites and were simply called al-Shurāt.[91] It is not clear, however, whether their adherence to Khārijism dates only from this period and whether it was more than a passing phase.[92]

At the moderate end of the scale of Khārijism stood the Ibāḍiyya. They considered non-Ibāḍī Muslims and sinners of their own community not as polytheists but merely as "infidels by ingratitude" (*kuffār niʿma*). As such it was licit to intermarry with them, to inherit from them, and their legal testimony, even against members of the Ibāḍī community, was valid. It was forbidden to kill or capture them in peacetime. In war their blood could be shed only after they had been summoned to the true faith, and only their weapons and horses were licit spoils. In spite of their status as infidels they were recognized as *muwaḥḥidūn,* confessors of the unity of God. The territory of the Muslim world at large was thus considered as *dār tawḥīd,* with the exception of the camp of the illegitimate government (*sulṭān*) which was *dār baghy,* abode of rebellion.[93] These views were obviously designed to facilitate relations of the Ibāḍīs with other Muslims and to allow their partial integration into the Muslim community. Although by no means quietists, the Ibāḍiyya generally were more reluctant than other Khārijites to take up arms. Rather, they were strongly engaged in religious scholarship and played a significant role in the early elaboration of legal and theological doctrine in Islam.

The great Ibāḍī revolts of the late Umayyad age and later took place

---

which was recommended practice (*sunna*), and dissociation from those denying God, which was obligatory duty (*farīḍa*).

90. See especially al-Shahrastānī, p. 102.

91. *Murūj,* §§ 1118, 1994. Besides the Shurāt, al-Masʿūdī mentions the Hadhbānī Kurds in Adharbayjan.

92. It may be noted, however, that the Khārijite Musāwir b. ʿAbd al-Ḥamīd revolting in the Mosul area in 252/866 was backed by many Kurds (Ibn al-Athīr, XII, p. 175).

93. Nashwān, p. 173; al-Baghdādī, *al-Farq,* p. 85; al-Shahrastānī, p. 100. Al-Ashʿarī, p. 104, l. 14, *dār kufr* may be a corruption of *dār baghy.*

in the Maghrib and Arabia. Among the Berbers in the Maghrib and in ʿOman Ibāḍī Khārijism gained its largest popular following and has survived there until the present. In Iran no Ibāḍī rebellions are recorded at any time. Yet there is evidence that Persians took a leading part in early Ibāḍism and that substantial Ibāḍī communities existed in regions of Iran in the late Umayyad and early ʿAbbasid ages.

A Persian was Abū ʿUbayda Muslim b. Abī Karīma, *mawlā* of Tamīm, the great leader of the Ibāḍiyya from 95/714 until his death during the caliphate of al-Manṣūr. His original name is variously given as Kūdīn, Kūzīn or Karzīn. He was a student of Jābir b. Zayd al-Azdī, the early Ibāḍī scholar and leader of the community in Basra. As a result of the Ibāḍī involvement in the rebellion of ʿAbd al-Raḥmān b. al-Ashʿath in 81–82/701–702, Abū ʿUbayda was imprisoned by al-Ḥajjāj. After his release by Yazīd b. al-Muhallab, he was elected as leader of the community in Basra in succession to Jābir. He was responsible for sending the so-called *ḥamalat al-ʿilm,* carriers of knowledge, taught by him to distant parts of the Muslim world.[94]

Among those Abū ʿUbayda sent to the Maghrib was the Persian ʿAbd al-Raḥmān b. Rustam (d. 168/784), founder of the Rustamid dynasty of Tāhart in Algeria. ʿAbd al-Raḥmān was born in Iraq but grew up in Qayrawān where his mother, remarrying after his father's death, took him. After having been won for Ibāḍism, he went to Basra to study under Abū ʿUbayda who later, ab. 140/757, sent him back to the Maghrib with four other *ḥamalat al-ʿilm.* When the Ibāḍī Berbers under their imam Abu l-Khaṭṭāb captured Qayrawān in 141/758, he became its governor. After the ʿAbbasids overthrew and killed Abu l-Khaṭṭāb in 144/761, he fled and established himself in Tāhart. Attempts to restore the Ibāḍī imamate in Tripolitania ended in failure, and ʿAbd al-Raḥmān was recognized as imam in Tāhart in 160/777 or 162/779. The dynasty founded by him lasted until 296/909.[95]

The revolt of the Ibāḍī caliph ʿAbd Allāh b. Yaḥyā Ṭālib al-Ḥaqq in Arabia toward the end of the Umayyad reign was actively backed by the Persian Qurʾan reader, grammarian and poet ʿAbd al-ʿAzīz Bishkast in Medina. Bishkast had been concealing his Khārijite convictions while teaching the Medinans Arabic grammar. When Abū Ḥamza al-Azdī occupied the town in the name of the Ibāḍī caliph in 130/747, he came forth as an enthusiastic supporter. After Abū

94. See T. Lewicki, art. "al-Ibāḍiyya" in *E.I.*, 2nd ed.
95. The Rustamids claimed royal Persian descent. See J. C. Wilkinson, "The Early Development of the Ibāḍī Movement in Baṣra," p. 130 and n. 16.

Ḥamza's defeat in battle by the Umayyad army, he was killed by the Medinans.[96]

Abū ʿUbayda also sent *ḥamalat al-ʿilm* to Khurasan. The first Ibāḍī missionary there is said to have been Hilāl b. ʿAṭiyya al-Khurāsānī.[97] Under Abū ʿUbayda's successor, al-Rabīʿ b. Ḥabīb, around the middle of the second/eighth century, Hāshim b. ʿAbd Allāh came from Khurasan to Basra and later returned carrying the doctrine of al-Rabīʿ to the Khurasanian Ibāḍīs. He is described as a legal scholar and *muftī*, of "the most pious people."[98] Other Ibāḍī legal scholars teaching in Khurasan at this time were Ḥātim b. Manṣūr and Abū Saʿīd ʿAbd Allāh b. ʿAbd al-ʿAzīz.[99] Both scholars deviated to some extent from the doctrine of al-Rabīʿ and were counted among the four jurists whose teaching was accepted as authoritative by the Nukkār, an Ibāḍī sect emerging during the early reign of the Rustamid imam ʿAbd al-Wahhāb b. ʿAbd al-Raḥmān (168–208/785–823) in the Maghrib.[100] Their views were frequently quoted by Abū Ghānim Bishr b. Ghānim al-Khurāsānī in his *Kitāb al-Mudawwana,* an important early work on Ibāḍī *fiqh.* Also living in Khurasan, Abū Ghānim visited Tāhart during the reign of imam ʿAbd al-Wahhāb and left a copy of his book in the Ibāḍī library there. He died perhaps around 230/845.[101] A biographical work of Bishr b. Ghānim was edited by a certain Abū Yazīd al-Khurāsānī, evidently one of his pupils in Khurasan.[102] Abū ʿĪsā Ibrāhīm b. Ismāʿīl al-Khurāsānī sent a *risāla* addressed to the Ibāḍī community in the Maghrib during, or shortly after, the reign of the Rustamid Aflaḥ b. ʿAbd al-Wahhāb (208–258?/823–872?). In the *risāla,* whose text is partly preserved, he backed, in the name of the Khurāsānī community, the Rustamid imams in a dispute with an Ibāḍī schismatic.[103]

These details indicate the presence of a sizable Ibāḍī community in

96. Abu l-Faraj al-Iṣfahānī, *al-Aghānī,* I, p. 114, XX, pp. 108–110; Ibn al-Qifṭī, *Inbāh al-ruwāt,* II, p. 183; Wellhausen, *Oppositionsparteien,* pp. 54–55.

97. Lewicki, "al-Ibāḍiyya."

98. Abū Ghānim al-Khurāsānī, *al-Mudawwana,* II, p. 276; Ibn Sallām al-Ibāḍī, *Badʾ al-Islām,* ed. W. Schwartz and al-Shaykh Sālim b. Yaʿqūb, p. 115.

99. See Abū Ghānim, *al-Mudawwana,* I, p. 205: *qāla Ḥātim b. Manṣūr wa-ghayruh min fuqahāʾ Khurāsān.* II, p. 231 Ḥātim b. Manṣūr is quoted as saying: *lā nazālu bi-khayrin mā dāma fīnā Abū Saʿīd* (ʿAbd Allāh b. ʿAbd al-ʿAzīz) *fa-lā naʾat ʿannā dāruhū wa-lā awḥashanā llāhu bi-faqdih.* Abū Saʿīd thus also lived in Khurasan.

100. Al-Shammākhī, *al-Siyar,* p. 280.

101. See T. Lewicki, art. "Abū Ghānim al-Khurāsānī" in *E.I.,* 2nd ed.; J. van Ess, "Untersuchungen zu einigen ibāḍitischen Handschriften," pp. 38–42.

102. van Ess, "Untersuchungen," p. 35, n. 26.

103. See Ibn Sallām, pp. 135–141.

Khurasan in the second/eighth and early third/ninth century. No information, however, is available about its precise location, ethnic composition, and later fate. It is also evident that the Ibāḍī community, unlike the ʿAjārida, was always oriented toward centers outside Iran, first in Basra and later in the Maghrib. There is also mention of an Ibāḍī scholar from Khwārazm, Abū Yazīd al-Khuwārazmī, a contemporary of ʿAbd al-Raḥmān b. Rustam.[104]

The heresiographers provide information on a deviant Ibāḍī sect, the Yazīdiyya, founded by the Basran Yazīd b. Unaysa who was active in Jūr (Gūr), the later Fīrūzābād, in Fars.[105] Yazīd taught that God would send in the future a prophet (*rasūl*) from among the non-Arabs (*ʿajam*) and would reveal to him a scripture written in heaven and, unlike the Qurʾan, sent down all at once. This scripture would abrogate the religious law of Muḥammad and bring a different one. The religion of this prophet would be that of the Sabians mentioned in the Qurʾan, who were different from the Sabians known at the present time. He taught furthermore that all people with a scripture (*ahl al-kitāb*) who testified to the prophethood of Muḥammad were true believers (*muʾminīn*) even if they did not enter his religion and did not act in accordance with his religious law, and professed association (*tawallā*) with them.

The great majority of the Ibāḍīs dissociated from Yazīd b. Unaysa, evidently considering his doctrines highly heretical.[105] He may well have been influenced, as has been argued by J. van Ess,[107] by the Jewish schismatic known to the Muslim heresiographers as Abū ʿĪsā al-Iṣfahānī, founder of the ʿĪsawiyya sect in Isfahan. Abū ʿĪsā claimed to be the messenger (*rasūl*) of the Messiah whose advent he predicted. He taught that there were five messengers of the Messiah who paved his way, among them Jesus and Muḥammad. Both were true prophets, although their missions, unlike the future mission of the Messiah, was not universal. Christians and Muslims were thus rightly guided believers like the Jews. The similarities of Abū ʿĪsā al-Iṣfahānī's and Yazīd b. Unaysa's doctrine are striking, and the latter may well have had the ʿĪsawiyya Jews in particular in mind as people of the book who confessed the prophethood of Muḥammad without adopting his

104. Ibn Sallām, p. 114; al-Shammākhī, p. 95.
105. For the following see J. van Ess, "Yazīd b. Unaisa und Abū ʿĪsā al-Iṣfahānī. Zur Konvergenz zweier sektiererischer Bewegungen."
106. See especially al-Ashʿarī, pp. 103–104; al-Baghdādī, *al-Farq*, pp. 263–264; al-Shahrastānī, pp. 101–102.
107. "Yazīd b. Unaisa."

religious law. Yazīd appears to have been active in the unsettled conditions before the fall of the Umayyad caliphate. Nothing is known about the further fate of his movement which probably disintegrated soon.

There was apparently still, however, an Ibāḍī community in eastern Fars during the fourth/tenth century. Al-Masʿūdī (d. 345/956) reports that the two towns of Harāt Iṣṭakhr and Ṣāhak (Chāhik), east of Iṣṭakhr near the border of Kirman, were inhabited by Khārijites.[108] Not much later al-Malaṭī (d. 377/987) describes the Khārijite community of the region of Harāt Iṣṭakhr in terms which strongly suggest that they were Ibāḍīs, although he calls them simply al-Shurāt. "The tenth sect of the Khārijites are the Shurāt who consider anyone committing acts of disobedience (*aṣḥāb al-maʿāṣī*), both minor and major sins, as infidels and dissociate from the two sons-in-law (*khatanayn*), ʿUthmān and ʿAlī, and back the two shaykhs, Abū Bakr and ʿUmar. They do not hold the seizure of the property of the people licit and do not enslave women, nor do they deviate (from the Sunnites) in any point of faith (*dīn*) or a sunna. They say that the sinners are infidels by ingratitude (*kuffār niʿma*), not infidels by polytheism (*kuffār shirk*). They live in the region of Harāt Iṣṭakhr between (?) and Kirmān. They have books composed by them in order to demonstrate the truth of their doctrine in which there are proofs and difficult discourse (*kalām ṣaʿb*). Among them there are scholars and jurists, and they possess distinct manliness (*muruwwa*), vast property, and abundance. Today the doctrines of the Muʿtazila have appeared among them, and some of them have abandoned their beliefs and have adopted Muʿtazilism."[109] The community probably disappeared by the end of the century.

108. *Murūj*, § 1994. *Harāh* read *Harāt* as suggested in the editor's footnote 8.

109. Al-Malaṭī, p. 43. The distinction between *kufr niʿma* and *kufr shirk* was distinctive for the Ibāḍiyya among the Khārijites. Al-Malaṭī listed the Ibāḍiyya earlier as a sect of the Khārijites without describing their doctrine.

Shiᶜism: The Imāmiyya and the Zaydiyya

Shiᶜism, the religious veneration of ᶜAlī and the Family of the Prophet, was born in Kufa in Iraq. It did not affect Iran until some time after the collapse of the Kufan Shiᶜite revolt under al-Mukhtār in favor of ᶜAlī's son Muḥammad b. al-Ḥanafiyya. One of the sectarian movements arising out of this revolt, the Hāshimiyya, was the first Shiᶜite group to disseminate its revolutionary message in Iran. By the end of the Umayyad age, a wave of revolutionary Shiᶜism of Kaysānī inspiration swept Iran and attracted a broad popular following. After the success of the revolution with the establishment of the ᶜAbbasid caliphate and the subsequent ᶜAbbasid volte-face in favor of Sunnism, this branch of the Shīᶜa disintegrated as quickly as it had risen, although some of its beliefs and aspirations remained alive among the Khurramiyya. Its popular character was reflected in the Persian romance of Abū Muslim, its martyred hero,[1] which could still in the eleventh/seventeenth century provoke an angry reaction among the Persian Imāmī Shiᶜite *ᶜulamā*ᵓ who had no sympathy for this ideological deviation.[2]

The next two Shiᶜite sectarian movements to enter the Iranian scene also had their roots in Kufa. A new stage in the development of Shiᶜism had begun there with the teaching of a grandson of al-Ḥusayn, Muḥammad al-Bāqir. In an age when the early Sunnite schools of religious law began to take shape, committed Kufan Shiᶜites turned to him to resolve disputed legal and other religious questions with the authority of the most learned member of the Family of the Prophet. Muḥammad al-Bāqir thus became the founder of Shiᶜite religious law.

A few years after al-Bāqir's death around 117/735, the Kufan Shīᶜa split about the question of backing the revolt of his brother Zayd b. ᶜAlī. The more radical of al-Bāqir's followers withdrew their support from Zayd when he refused to condemn the first two caliphs unequivocally as unjust usurpers of the rights of ᶜAlī. They attached themselves to al-Bāqir's son Jaᶜfar al-Ṣādiq as their imam under whose leadership the Imāmiyya emerged as a religious community with a distinctive law, ritual, and theological doctrine. As the Kaysāniyya and its various branches disintegrated after the rise of the ᶜAbbasids, the Imāmiyya became heir to much of its radical Shiᶜite teaching.

Jaᶜfar al-Ṣādiq developed in the law the pronouncements of his fa-

1. See I. Mélikoff, *Le "porte-hache" du Khorasan dans la tradition épique turco-iranienne.*
2. Ḡ. H. Yūsofī, "Abū Moslem K̲orāsānī," in *E. Ir.*

ther into a comprehensive system. Constitutive for the Imāmī community, however, was his doctrine of the imamate. This was based on the belief that mankind is at all times in need of a divinely appointed and guided leader and teacher in all matters of religion. Imam Jaʿfar affirmed that the world could never exist even for a moment without such a leader. In order to be able to fulfill his divine mission, he must be endowed with perfect immunity (*ʿiṣma*) from error and sin. After the age of the prophets came to an end with Muḥammad, the imams as his heirs would continue the prophetic mission in every respect except that they would not bring a new scripture. The imamate thus was raised to the rank of prophethood. Rejection, disobedience, or ignorance of any of the divinely invested imams was infidelity equal to the rejection of the Prophet. The great majority of the Companions of Muḥammad had thus apostatized from Islam when they accepted the caliphate of Abū Bakr and ignored the divinely ordained designation of ʿAlī by the Prophet as his legatee (*waṣī*) and successor. Most of the Muslim community continued to live in this state of apostasy. After ʿAlī the line of rightful imams had passed through his sons Ḥasan and Ḥusayn and the descendants of the latter to Jaʿfar al-Ṣādiq, the sixth imam. It would continue to be handed down from father to son until the end of time.

Although the imams were the only legitimate rulers of the Muslim community, their imamate did not depend on actual reign or an active attempt to gain it. Imam Jaʿfar did not aspire to rule and strictly forbade his followers to engage in revolutionary activity. He predicted that the imams would not regain their rightful position until one of them would eventually rise as the Qāʾim who would rule the world. The antirevolutionary quietism of this vision of the near future was reinforced by imam Jaʿfar's insistence on the practice of *taqiyya,* precautionary dissimulation of religious beliefs, which he imposed on his followers as a fundamental duty of faith under the present conditions. These elements in his teaching neutralized to some extent its radical repudiation of the established caliphate and thus improved the chances of survival in the hostile environment of a nominally Muslim community whose conduct it utterly condemned.

The great majority of imam Jaʿfar's followers were Kufans. Imāmī Shiʿism spread, however, already in his lifetime to Qom, its earliest and most stable home in Iran. Qom was a pre-Islamic town conquered by the Arabs under Abū Mūsā al-Ashʿarī around 23/644. More than sixty years later the town and its environs were chosen by a clan of Ashʿar from Kufa as a haven of refuge from the awesome Umayyad governor al-Ḥajjāj. According to one account, the sons of Saʿd b. Mālik b. ʿĀmir al-Ashʿarī, ʿAbd Allāh al-Aḥwaṣ, ʿAbd al-Raḥmān, Isḥāq, and Nuʿaym, had participated in the great revolt of ʿAbd al-Raḥmān b. al-Ashʿath and fled after his defeat in Iraq to Iran. They took possession of some villages in the environs of Qom by force, killing many of the people, and settled there. Another account dates their arrival ten years later in 94/713 and pictures their settlement as more peaceful.[3] The sons of Saʿd b. Mālik al-Ashʿarī, members of the South-Arabian tribal aristocracy of Kufa, evidently brought with them their numerous dependents and retinue. Their descendants were to dominate Qom for the next three centuries.

When they first settled in Qom, the Banū Saʿd b. Mālik were anti-Umayyad but not Shiʿite, at least not in any sectarian sense. At the time of the ʿAbbasid revolution, they joined Qaḥṭaba b. Shabīb, the ʿAbbasid commander, in Gorgan to help in the overthrow of the hated Umayyad dynasty.[4] Yet a few decades later most of them had become staunch Imāmī Shiʿites. The first one among them to become a follower of imam Jaʿfar is said to have been a son of ʿAbd Allāh b. Saʿd b. Mālik, most likely ʿĪsā b. ʿAbd Allāh. ʿĪsā is mentioned in the Imāmī *rijāl* books as a transmitter from imam Jaʿfar and his son Mūsā al-Kāẓim and as the author of some questions which he put to imam ʿAlī al-Riḍā.[5] The other members of the family seem to have followed his lead. Not all of his generation, however, became Shiʿites. Ibn Saʿd mentions two Sunnite traditionists of Qom from among them, Ashʿath b. Isḥāq b. Saʿd and Yaʿqūb b. ʿAbd Allāh, a brother of ʿĪsā. The rigorously Sunnite traditionist Jarīr b. ʿAbd Allāh, *qāḍī* of Ray, is reported to have said whenever he met Yaʿqūb: "This is the believer among the family of Pharaoh (*hādhā muʾmin āl Firʿawn*)."[6] The rest of the clan thus was definitely Shiʿite before the death of Yaʿqūb in 174/790–791.

By the end of the second/eighth century Qom was, like Kufa, solidly Shiʿite and, unlike Kufa, solidly Imāmī. In Kufa the Shīʿa was deeply divided into many rival factions enumerated in the books on the sects of the Shīʿa. The majority of the Kufans inclined to Zaydī rather than Imāmī Shiʿism. More seriously, the Imāmiyya split up after the death

3. Yāqūt, *Muʿjam al-buldān,* IV, pp. 175–176; Ḥasan b. Muḥammad b. Ḥasan Qummī, *Tārīkh-i Qumm,* ed. Jalāl al-Dīn Tihrānī, pp. 242ff.

4. *Tārīkh-i Qumm,* p. 260.

5. Al-Najāshī, *al-Rijāl,* p. 228; al-Ṭusi, *K. Fihrist kutub al-shīʿa,* ed. A. Sprenger and Mawlawy ʿAbd al-Ḥaqq, p. 228.

6. Ibn Saʿd, VII/2, pp. 110–111; Ibn Ḥajar, *Tahdhīb al-tahdhīb,* I, p. 350, XI, pp. 390–391.

of Ja'far al-Ṣādiq. Some of his followers denied his death and expected his return while some others considered Muḥammad, son of his predeceased eldest son Ismā'īl, the legitimate imam. The bulk of his Kufan followers, however, first recognized his eldest surviving son, 'Abd Allāh al-Afṭaḥ, as the successor. When 'Abd Allāh died a few months later without leaving a son, they turned to his brother Mūsā al-Kāẓim, the seventh imam of the Twelver Shī'a. Many of them, however, continued to recognize 'Abd Allāh as the rightful imam before Mūsā. They were known as the Faṭḥiyya and constituted a sizable faction in Kufa until the late fourth/tenth century. In the third/ninth century some of the most important Imāmī traditionists in the town, like the Banū Faḍḍāl, were Faṭḥīs. Al-Ḥasan b. 'Alī b. Faḍḍāl (d. ab. 220/835 or 224/839), a client of the Banū Taym Allāh was a major transmitter from Mūsā al-Kāẓim.[7] Although it was claimed that he disavowed the imamate of 'Abd Allāh al-Afṭaḥ on his deathbed, this was denied by his son Aḥmad (d. 260/874), also a Faṭḥī traditionist and author.[8] Al-Ḥasan's younger son 'Alī is described by the Twelver Shi'ite al-Najāshī as the "jurisconsult of our companions in Kufa, their leader and their expert in *ḥadīth*." Yet he, too, was a Faṭḥī and wrote a book in affirmation of the imamate of 'Abd Allāh al-Afṭaḥ (*Kitāb ithbāt imāmat 'Abd Allāh*).[9]

Even more serious was the schism among the followers of imam Mūsā after he died in prison in Baghdad in 183/799. Many denied his death and claimed that he would return as the Mahdī attributing special significance to his being the seventh imam. They did not recognize 'Alī al-Riḍā, the eighth imam of the Twelver Shī'a, though some of them considered him and his descendants as lieutenants (*khulafā'*) of the Mahdī during his absence. Many, perhaps the majority, of the Kufan Imāmī transmitters in the third/ninth century belonged to this sect, known as the Wāqifa. Most prominent among them were the Banū Samā'a, Muḥammad b. Samā'a b. Mūsā, his sons al-Ḥasan (d. 263/877), Ibrāhīm and Ja'far and his grandson Mu'allā b. al-Ḥasan.[10] Aside from this schism, the Kufan Imāmiyya was also plagued by the activity in their midst of prominent extremists (*ghulāt*) like al-Mufaḍḍal b. 'Umar,[11] Muḥammad b. Sinān (d. 220/835)[12] and

7. Al-Najāshī, pp. 26–28; al-Ṭūsī, *Fihrist,* pp. 93–94.
8. Al-Najāshī, pp. 62–63; al-Ṭūsī, *Fihrist,* pp. 25–26.
9. Al-Najāshī, pp. 195–196; al-Ṭūsī, *Fihrist,* p. 216.
10. Al-Najāshī, pp. 252–253, 32–33, 92; al-Ṭūsī, *Fihrist,* pp. 97–98.
11. Al-Najāshī, p. 326; H. Halm, "Das 'Buch der Schatten,'" in *Der Islam,* LV, pp. 224ff.
12. Al-Najāshī, pp. 251–252; Halm, "Das 'Buch der Schatten,'" pp. 236ff.

Abū Sumayna Muḥammad b. ʿAlī al-Ṣayrafī[13] who escaped excommunication by the imams.

In Qom the Shīʿa were united in their allegiance to the line of imams of orthodox Twelver Shiʿism. There is no mention of any Faṭḥī or Wāqifī deviation among the numerous Imāmī traditionists of the town. The leaders of the Ashāʿira, who controlled the town with the backing of the ʿAbbasid government, also acted as guardians of Imāmī orthodoxy. After ʿĪsā b. ʿAbd Allāh b. Saʿd his son Abū ʿAlī Muḥammad is described by al-Najāshī as the shaykh of the Qummīs, the chief of the Ashāʿira, and as prestigious with the government (*mutaqaddim ʿind al-sulṭān*). He visited imam ʿAlī al-Riḍā and related from imam Muḥammad al-Jawād.[14] After him his son Abū Jaʿfar Aḥmad b. Muḥammad b. ʿĪsā b. ʿAbd Allāh succeeded to the leadership. He was, according to al-Najāshī, the shaykh of the Qummīs, their chief, their undisputed jurisconsult, and also the *raʾīs* who would meet the government as the representative of the town. He visited the imams al-Riḍā, al-Jawād, and ʿAlī al-Hādī.[15] His word was decisive in judging transmitters inclining to *ghuluww*. Thus he did not transmit from al-Ḥasan b. Khurrazādh, a traditionist from Qom who became an extremist toward the end of his life.[16] He testified against Sahl b. ʿAlī al-Rāzī that he was a *ghālī* and a liar and expelled him from Qom to his hometown Ray.[17] The Kufan extremist Muḥammad b. ʿAlī al-Ṣayrafī stayed with him in Qom for a while. When his extremist teaching became public, however, he was forced to go into hiding and then was banished by Aḥmad b. Muḥammad from the town.[18] Aḥmad b. Muḥammad b. Khālid al-Barqī, a prolific Imāmī traditionist and author from Barqarūd near Qom, was also driven out of Qom by Aḥmad b. Muḥammad b. ʿĪsā because he transmitted from weak transmitters. Later, however, the latter permitted him to return and apologized to him. When al-Barqī died in 274/887 or 280/893 he joined the funeral procession barefoot and bareheaded.[19]

Qom thus became the chief center of orthodox Imāmī traditionism in the third/ninth century. It was here that the traditions of the imams first transmitted in Kufa and elsewhere were sifted and collected. An

13. Al-Najāshī, pp. 255–256; Halm, "Das 'Buch der Schatten,'" pp. 241–242.
14. Al-Najāshī, p. 261.
15. Al-Najāshī, pp. 64–65; al-Ṭūsī, *Fihrist*, pp. 26–27.
16. Al-Najāshī, pp. 35, 64.
17. Al-Najāshī, p. 140.
18. Al-Najāshī, p. 255; al-Ṭūsī, *Fihrist*, p. 302.
19. Ibn Muṭahhar al-Ḥillī, *Rijāl al-ʿAllāma al-Ḥillī*, ed. Muḥ. Ṣādiq Āl Baḥr al-ʿUlūm, pp. 14–15.

examination of the chains of transmission in the canonical collections of Twelver Shiʿite traditions will provide full evidence for this.[20] In the most famous one, the *Kitāb al-Kāfī* of al-Kulaynī, over 80 percent of all traditions were related from traditionists of Qom. If traditions transmitted by scholars of al-Kulaynī's hometown Ray, who were in close touch with the traditionists of Qom, are added, their proportion reaches well above 90 percent. Ibn-Bābawayh al-Ṣadūq, himself a leading representative of the school of Qom, in his *Kitāb Man lā yaḥḍuruhu l-faqīh* related nearly exclusively from traditionists of his hometown.

The contribution of Qom to the development of Twelver Shiʿism both by sheltering the main center of Imāmī traditionist learning and by uncompromisingly adhering to the line of the Twelve Imams thus was weighty. Without it Twelver Shiʿism might never have become the predominant form of Shiʿism. It must be noted, however, that Qom and its Imāmī scholarship in this period were dominated by Arabs, in particular the Ashāʿira. The great majority of the traditionists of Qom, especially the most prominent ones, were Arabs in contrast to Kufa, where the majority of the Imāmī traditionists were *mawālī*. Aḥmad b. Muḥammad b. ʿĪsā al-Ashʿarī, the chief of the town and the scholars of Qom, was a proud Arab and wrote a book on the virtues of the Arabs (*Kitāb Faḍāʾil al-ʿArab*).[21] After the death of imam Muḥammad al-Jawād in 220/825 he initially refused to confirm the appointment of ʿAlī al-Hādī as his successor when it was made public by the Persian al-Khayrānī, although he had been privy to the secret. Challenged by al-Khayrānī, he admitted that he knew of the appointment, adding that he had wished that the honor of making the announcement would have gone to an Arab rather than a Persian.[22]

In the course of the fourth/tenth century, the school of Qom was eclipsed by the rise of the Imāmī *kalām* school of Baghdad which espoused rational theology and legal methodology against uncritical adherence to tradition.[23] The Shaykh al-Mufīd (d. 413/1022), its first leader, openly turned against Ibn Bābawayh al-Ṣadūq, the chief representative of the school of Qom and his teacher, and wrote a correction (*taṣḥīḥ*) to his creed. There he referred to the scholars of Qom as the Ḥashwiyya (a contemptuous designation of Sunnite traditionalists) of the Shīʿa and brushed off their claim of being the guardians of Twelver Shiʿite orthodoxy. His pupil and successor, the Sharīf al-Mur-

20. See "The Sources of Ismāʿīlī Law," p. 31.
21. Al-Najāshī, p. 64.
22. Al-Kulaynī, *al-Uṣūl min al-Kāfī*, ed. ʿAlī Akbar al-Ghaffārī, I, p. 324.
23. See "Imamism and Muʿtazilite Theology," pp. 21ff.

taḍā ʿAlam al-Hudā (d. 436/1044) carried rationalism a step further insisting, like the Muʿtazila, that reason alone, unaided by revelation, must discover the fundamentals of religion. He was even more contemptuous of the scholars of Qom than al-Mufīd. With the single exception of Ibn Bābawayh, they were, he affirmed, all anthropomorphists and predestinarians, not to mention their other heretical doctrines. Thus they were as unacceptable as transmitters of tradition as were their Sunnite counterparts. Their books were indeed full of obvious forgeries. Al-Murtaḍā did not even exclude al-Kulaynī's *Kitāb al-Kāfī,* usually considered the most authoritative of Twelver Shiʿite *ḥadīth* collections, from this devastating judgment. In order to escape the need of relying on the objectionable traditions of the Imāmī traditionists, al-Murtaḍā proposed to build the Imāmī law on the principle of consensus (*ijmāʿ*). The result was evidently not convincing, and only few later Imāmī scholars followed his legal doctrine, whereas his theological views prevailed until the beginning of the Mongol age. His pupil, the Shaykh al-Ṭāʾifa al-Ṭūsī (d. 460/1067), argued that many of the traditions of the Imāmī traditionists, though technically *āḥād,* singly transmitted, and thus not acceptable on rational principles, were in fact covered by the consensus since they had been universally used by the Imāmī community in the presence of the imams and with their approval. Al-Ṭūsī thus in effect rehabilitated the school of Qom, at least partially. The traditions of the imams transmitted and collected by it were no longer ultimate authority, but they were primary source material for the systematic Twelver Shiʿite law which al-Ṭūsī elaborated on the basis of his legal methodology. In theology al-Ṭūsī followed uncompromisingly the rationalist doctrine of al-Murtaḍā.

The school of Qom disintegrated in the fifth/eleventh century. Its traditionalist outlook remained latent until it was powerfully restated by Muḥammad b. Amīn al-Astarābādī, the founder of the Akhbārī school, in the eleventh/seventeenth century. The main center of Twelver Shiʿite scholarship was moved from Baghdad when Shaykh al-Ṭūsī, no longer feeling safe in the hostile environment of the ʿAbbasid capital, moved to Najaf. In the sixth/twelfth century al-Ḥilla, on the route from Baghdad to Kufa, became the main center of Imāmī scholarship, now based largely on the work of al-Ṭūsī, and remained so during and beyond the Mongol age.

In Iran proper, the Twelver Shīʿa was now widely dispersed, though mostly in small minority communities. The origins of some of these communities are to be dated still in the time of the presence of the imams, the first half of the third/ninth century or even earlier. They were apparently influenced by, and oriented toward, Qom more so than Kufa. Nowhere in Iran is there any evidence of the Faṭḥī and Wāqifī heresies which were so prominent in Iraq. Several Imāmī traditionists were active already in this early time in Ahvaz in Khuzistan.[24] The Imāmī community in Ray and its environs also goes back to this period. Its focus came to be the tomb and later shrine of the Sayyid ʿAbd al-ʿAẓīm al-Ḥasanī, a companion of imams Muḥammad al-Jawād and ʿAlī al-Hādī, who came to the town about the middle of the third/ninth century and taught and died there.[25] Aside from Qom, Ray probably housed the most substantial Imāmī community in Iran during the Buwayhid and Saljūq age. Ābah near Sāvah was solidly Shiʿite from an early date. In Nishapur Imāmī Shiʿism was given a major boost by the activity of al-Faḍl b. Shādhān (d. ab. 260/874), a prominent Imāmī traditionist, legal scholar, *kalām* theologian, and prolific author with independent views. He was noted and criticized in particular for his use of reasoning in law and theology. His numerous books and his teaching were transmitted by his disciple ʿAlī b. Muḥammad b. Qutayba al-Naysābūrī.[26] In the fourth/tenth century the unorthodox outlook of the Twelver Shiʿite community of Nishapur was reaffirmed when it welcomed and honored the jurist Abū ʿAlī b. al-Junayd, who was ostracized by the schools of Baghdad and Qom for his advocacy of the use of analogy (*qiyās*) and speculative reasoning (*raʾy*) in the law.[27]

Still further east in Transoxania, Imamism also developed along an independent line in the fourth/tenth century. In Samarqand it was disseminated, after modest beginnings in the later third/ninth century, by Muḥammad b. Masʿūd al-ʿAyyāshī, a prominent and wealthy convert active in the early decades of the fourth/tenth century. Before his

24. ʿAbd Allāh b. Ghunaym al-Najāshī, governor of al-Ahwāz under the caliph al-Manṣūr and ancestor of the author of the *K. al-Rijāl,* is reported to have received and transmitted a *risāla* of imam Jaʿfar (al-Najāshī, pp. 79, 157). Al-Ḥusayn b. Saʿīd b. Ḥammād b. Mihrān al-Ahwāzī and his brother al-Ḥasan, first half of the third/ninth century, are known as the authors of the "Thirty Books" (al-Najāshī, pp. 46–48; al-Ṭūsī, *al-Fihrist,* pp. 104–105). ʿAbd Allāh b. Muḥammad b. al-Ḥusayn al-Ahwāzī transmitted *masāʾil* he had put to imam ʿAlī al-Riḍā (al-Najāshī, p. 168; al-Ṭūsī, *Fihrist,* p. 95). ʿAlī b. Mahziyār al-Ahwāzī transmitted from ʿAlī al-Riḍā and Muḥammad al-Jawād and wrote a large number of books (al-Najāshī, pp. 191–192; al-Ṭūsī, *Fihrist,* pp. 231–232).

25. "ʿAbd al-ʿAẓīm al-Ḥasanī," in *E. Ir.*

26. Al-Najāshī, pp. 255–256, 197; al-Ṭūsī, *Fihrist,* pp. 254–255.

27. Al-Najāshī, pp. 299–302; al-Ṭūsī, *Fihrist,* pp. 267–269; al-Mufīd, *al-Masāʾil al-Ṣāghāniyya,* in *ʿIddat rasāʾil li l-shaykh . . . al-Mufīd,* pp. 249ff. and *al-Masāʾil al-Sarawiyya,* ibid., pp. 222–225.

conversion to Shiᶜism, still a young man, he had acquired a vast knowledge of Sunnite *ḥadīth.* Later he continued to hold teaching sessions for Sunnites besides his sessions for the Shiᶜites. His numerous books were popular in northeastern Iran but were generally shunned by the Imāmīs in Iraq and western Iran who accused him of transmitting from weak informants (*ḍuᶜafāʾ*).[28] These weak informants were probably not so much unreliable Imāmī traditionists than men of a more diffuse Shiᶜism or merely Shiᶜite tendencies from whom strict Imāmī traditionists would not relate. One of the numerous students of al-ᶜAyyāshī was Abū ᶜAmr Muḥammad b. ᶜUmar al-Kashshī or al-Kishshī from the town of Kishsh in Transoxania. His book on the Shiᶜite traditionists had to be purged by the Shaykh al-Ṭūsī of the many entries on traditionists whom the latter considered as belonging to the *ᶜāmma,* the Sunnites, before it could be accepted by the orthodox Twelver Shiᶜites as one of their four basic early *rijāl* works.[29] Another pupil of al-ᶜAyyāshī, Abū Naṣr Aḥmad b. Yaḥyā of Samarqand, according to al-Ṭūsī used to give *fatwā*s to the *ᶜāmma,* here presumably meaning the Ḥanafites, according to their own doctrine, to the Ḥashwiyya, the Sunnite traditionalists, according to their teaching, and to the Shīᶜa, according to theirs.[30] It is not known how long al-ᶜAyyāshī's school survived.

A presence of Shiᶜites going back to the early third/ninth century is also indicated by the *nisba*s of early Imāmī traditionists and theologians in Balkh, Kashan, Qazvin, Gorgan, and Amol in Ṭabaristān. Ṭūs presumably harbored an Imāmī community ever since the eighth imam ᶜAlī al-Riḍā was buried there in 203/818. It did not become significant, however, until the fourth/tenth century. In Bayhaq (Sabzavār) the Imāmī community appears to date from that century. Other names of towns of progressively less importance for the early Shīᶜa could be added. The first Twelver Shiᶜite Iranian dynasty were the Bāvandids ruling Mazandaran in the Saljūq age where they acted as protectors and patrons of Imāmī scholars. At least some of the members of this dynasty in the fourth/tenth century, when their rule was still confined to the mountains, were also Twelver Shiᶜites, while at the beginning of that century the dynasty was still staunchly Sunnite.[31] The Buwayhids, sometimes considered the first Twelver Shiᶜite Ira-

28. Ibn al-Nadīm, *al-Fihrist,* ed. G. Flügel, pp. 194–195; al-Najāshī, pp. 270–273; al-Ṭūsī, *Fihrist,* pp. 317–320.
29. "Al-Kashshī," in *E.I.,* 2nd ed.
30. Al-Ṭūsī, *Rijāl,* ed. Muḥ. Ṣādiq Āl Baḥr al-ᶜUlūm, pp. 439, 520.
31. See "Āl-e Bāvand," in *E. Ir.*

nian dynasty, were initially rather Zaydīs and later tended to back Muʿtazilism and Shiʿism with no allegiance to a specific branch. Twelver Shiʿism thus was well established throughout much of Iran before the Mongol conquest. Yet it predominated in very few and only minor towns and regions except for Qom. Altogether it constituted a small minority in a Sunnite country. This did not substantially change in the Mongol and Timurid age in spite of some local expansion of Shiʿism. At the time of the rise of the Safavids Mashhad, the home of the most sacred shrine of the Shīʿa in Iran, was still a predominantly Sunnite town.[32] Twelver Shiʿism was eventually imposed on Iran by a decision of government. It did not impose itself on government by its popularity and spread among the people.

The other branch of the Shīʿa which arose from the revolt of Zayd b. ʿAlī in Kufa affected Iran later and more marginally than the Imāmiyya. The Zaydiyya, backers of his revolt, essentially retained the politically militant but religiously moderate attitude predominant in the early Kufan Shīʿa. They developed a doctrine of the imamate distinctly at variance with that of the Imāmiyya. They neither accepted a hereditary line of imams nor considered the imam as divinely protected from sin and error. Rather they held that any descendant of Ḥasan or Ḥusayn qualified by religious learning could claim the imamate by armed rising against the illegitimate rulers and was entitled to the allegiance and active support of the faithful. Thus there could be long periods without a legitimate Zaydī imam. In the absence of any ʿAlid claimant possessing the high qualifications of religious learning, the Zaydīs often backed ʿAlid rulers as mere *dāʿīs*, summoners, who were defined by late legal theory as imams with restricted competence.[33]

In their condemnation of the Muslim community at large the Zaydīs were less radical than the Imāmiyya. While they mostly agreed with them that ʿAlī, Ḥasan, and Ḥusayn had been invested as imams by the Prophet, they rejected the Imāmī thesis that the designation (*naṣṣ*) had been clear and unambiguous. Rather it had been obscure so that its meaning could be discovered only by investigation. Thus they minimized the offense of the Companions and the early Muslim com-

32. This is evident from Ibn Abi l-Jumhūr al-Aḥsāʾī's account of his discussions in Mashhad with a Sunnite scholar from Herat in 878/1474 (*al-Risāla al-mawsūma bi l-mubāḥatha bayn al-muḥiqq wa l-mubṭil = Munāẓarat al-Harawī,* ms. Tehran Majlis 3246, pp. 137ff.)

33. R. Strothmann, *Das Staatsrecht der Zaiditen,* pp. 94ff.; *Der Imam al-Qāsim,* pp. 154–156.

munity in ignoring it and backing the caliphate of ʿAlī's predecessors. With their strong revolutionary motivation, however, they were close to the Khārijites and posed a more immediate threat to the established caliphate and the peace of the community than the quietist Imāmiyya. They were thus subject to more vigorous suppression and, like the Khārijites, could succeed only in inaccessible regions far from the centers of caliphal power.

Although some abortive early revolts of Zaydī imams took place on Iranian soil, sectarian Zaydism did not take roots there for about a century after the death of Zayd b. ʿAlī in 122/740. Zayd's son Yaḥyā, who is counted by the Zaydīs as one of their imams, found much sympathy and some support in Khurasan where he fled after the failure of the Kufan revolt in favor of his father. He was given shelter in various places while being pursued by the Umayyad authorities until he was tracked down and killed near Jūzjān in 125/743. His local backing was mostly orchestrated, however, by the ʿAbbasid *daʿwa* which used his and his father's death to stir up anti-Umayyad sentiments without having much sympathy for their cause. Five decades later, under the early reign of Hārūn al-Rashīd, the Ḥasanid Yaḥyā b. ʿAbd Allāh, who had participated in the rebellion of the Ḥusaynid al-Ḥusayn b. ʿAlī in the Ḥijāz, found refuge with the Justānid king of the Daylamites in Rūdbār in the mountains of Daylamān. With him was a group of Kufan Zaydī supporters. The Daylamites were not yet converted to Islam, and there is no evidence that his brief stay before his surrender to the Barmakid al-Faḍl b. Yaḥyā opened the region to effective Zaydī penetration. In 219/834, shortly after the succession of al-Muʿtaṣim to the caliphate, the Ḥasanid Muḥammad b. al-Qāsim came to Ṭāliqān in Khurasan accompanied by a small group of Kufan Zaydīs and led a rebellion there which was quickly suppressed. There are no indications that any of his local backers were sectarian Zaydīs.

Zaydī teaching was first spread in Iran by some followers of the Ḥasanid imam al-Qāsim b. Ibrāhīm al-Rassī (d. 246/860), who lived and taught on the Jabal al-Rass east of Medina.[34] In his works there is mention of some Ṭabarīs putting questions on religious matters to him. One of the main transmitters of his legal doctrine was Jaʿfar b. Muḥammad al-Nayrūsī al-Ṭabarī, whose hometown Nayrūs was located in the mountains of western Ṭabaristān a few miles east of the Chālūs river. Western Ṭabaristān, the region of Rūyān, Kalār, and Chālūs became the first base of the Zaydiyya in Iran. In 250/864, four

34. *Der Imam al-Qāsim*, pp. 86ff.

years after the death of al-Qāsim b. Ibrāhīm, the people of this region revolted against the Ṭāhirid government and, on the advice of a local ʿAlid, invited the Ḥasanid al-Ḥasan b. Zayd from Ray to assume their leadership. Al-Ḥasan quickly gained control over all of Ṭabaristān and ruled with the regnal name al-Dāʿī ila l-Ḥaqq. He established his capital in Amol near the region from which most of his backing came. His brother and successor Muḥammad b. Zayd was killed in battle by the Sāmānids in 287/900 who restored Sunnite rule in Ṭabaristān.

In his religious policy al-Ḥasan b. Zayd officially imposed Shiʿite ritual and law and Muʿtazilī theology. Muḥammad evidently followed him and employed two prominent Muʿtazilī theologians, Abu l-Qāsim al-Balkhī and Abū Muslim al-Iṣfahānī, as his secretaries. Ibn al-Nadīm mentions the titles of some books on law and the imamate by al-Ḥasan. They are not extant, however, and are never mentioned or quoted in later Zaydī literature. Neither of the two brothers was recognized later as a Zaydī imam and they were accused of injustice, in particular by the followers of al-Qāsim b. Ibrāhīm's grandson Yaḥyā al-Hādī ila l-Ḥaqq, the founder of the Zaydī imamate in Yaman. Al-Hādī indeed visited Amol during the reign of Muḥammad b. Zayd, some time before his appearance in Yaman. Since he permitted his followers to address him as the imam, he became suspect to the ruler and was forced to leave precipitously. The Zaydīs of the school of al-Qāsim b. Ibrāhīm in Ṭabaristān evidently looked to his grandson as their authority in religious matters even though they backed the reign of al-Ḥasan and Muḥammad. A fair number of Ṭabarī Zaydīs joined al-Hādī after his rising in Yaman and became some of his most loyal supporters.

Zaydī ʿAlid rule in Ṭabaristān was restored in 301/914 by al-Ḥasan b. ʿAlī al-Uṭrūsh al-Nāṣir li l-Ḥaqq. A Ḥusaynid originally from Medina, he had come to Ṭabaristān during the reign of al-Ḥasan b. Zayd and participated in the battle in which Muḥammad b. Zayd was killed. He escaped to Ray and soon followed an invitation of the Justānid king of the Daylamites who promised him support in the reconquest of Ṭabaristān. After the failure of two initial campaigns to Ṭabaristān, al-Nāṣir settled down to convert those Daylamites who had not yet joined the Zaydī cause and the Gīlites east of the Safīdrūd to Islam. His religious doctrine differed in some points from that of al-Qāsim b. Ibrāhīm even though he considered the latter as one of his authorities. In the law in particular he was much more influenced by Imāmī doctrine than were al-Qāsim and al-Hādī. Thus he adopted the Imāmī rules concerning divorce and inheritance and the ritual ablution of the feet. As a result of these differences, his converts came to form a separate Zaydī community known as the Nāṣiriyya in distinction to the Qāsimiyya, the adherents of the school of al-Qāsim and al-Hādī prevalent in Rūyān and eastern Daylamān. With his new followers al-Nāṣir succeeded in wresting Ṭabaristān from the Sāmānids. Three years later, in 304/917, he died and was buried in Amol where his shrine became a place of pilgrimage for the Nāṣiriyya. They ever retained a strong attachment to his descendants and preferred them to other ʿAlids as candidates for the imamate.

The presence of two Zaydī schools in the Caspian provinces soon led to severe partisan strife between them. It was evidently furthered by the traditional ethnic antagonism between the Daylamites and the Gīlites, since the majority of the former belonged to the Qāsimiyya while all the Gīlites east of the Safīdrūd had become Nāṣiriyya. The situation was further complicated by the ties between the Qāsimiyya with the Zaydī community in Yaman with whom they agreed in doctrine and by their recognition of some of the Yamanite imams, while the Nāṣiriyya were confined to the Caspian region. In the heat of their rivalry extremists on both sides went so far as to declare the followers of the other school infidels and heretics. Around the middle of the fourth/tenth century the imam Abū ʿAbd Allāh al-Mahdī, who personally belonged to the Qāsimiyya but ruled in Hawsam (modern Rūdsar), the main center of Nāṣirī scholarship, endeavored to extinguish the partisan zeal by declaring both school doctrines as equally valid since both were based on the *ijtihād* of legitimate imams. While this opinion became the generally accepted view among the Caspian Zaydīs, this did not overcome the division completely. The continued existence of the two schools, combined with ethnic division and local patriotism, resulted in a more or less permanent political division of the Caspian Zaydī community. ʿAlid rule, after its collapse in Ṭabaristān and its restoration further west, was most of the time divided into a Daylamite and a Gīlite branch.

The Zaydiyya reached its peak in Iran in the Buwayhid age. The Buwayhids, Daylamites from the region of Lāhījān, first rose to leadership serving in the armies of the ʿAlids al-Nāṣir li l-Ḥaqq and his successor al-Ḥasan b. al-Qāsim al-Dāʿī. Although they later as rulers supported the ʿAbbasid caliphate for reasons of political expediency they protected and patronized Zaydī ʿAlids and furthered ʿAlid rule in their Caspian homeland. Abū ʿAbd Allāh al-Mahdī, the son of al-Ḥasan b. al-Qāsim al-Dāʿī and later Zaydī imam, was highly honored by the Buwayhid Muʿizz al-Dawla and was appointed syndic of the

ʿAlids in Baghdad with the extraordinary privilege of never having to dress on official occasions in black, the official color of the ʿAbbasids, or to attend the court of the caliph. Muʿizz al-Dawla is said to have privately referred to him as his own imam.

The two most famous scholars among the Caspian Zaydī imams after al-Nāṣir, the brothers Aḥmad b. al-Ḥusayn al-Muʾayyad bi llāh (d. 411/1020) and Abū Ṭālib Yaḥyā al-Nāṭiq bi l-Ḥaqq of the Buṭḥānī family, belonged both for some time to the circle of the Buwayhid vizier al-Ṣāḥib b. ʿAbbād in Ray and of his Muʿtazilī chief judge ʿAbd al-Jabbār al-Hamadhānī. The two brothers were born in Amol of an Imāmī father and became Zaydīs under the influence of their teacher Abu l-ʿAbbās al-Ḥasanī, a major representative of the school of al-Hādī in Ṭabaristān.[35] They studied Muʿtazilī theology in Baghdad under Abū ʿAbd Allāh al-Baṣrī, who had also taught Abū ʿAbd Allāh al-Mahdī. Abū ʿAbd Allāh al-Baṣrī was the head of the Basran school of the Muʿtazila before ʿAbd al-Jabbār, and through him the three Zaydī imams adopted the Basran Muʿtazilī theology while al-Hādī had been closer to the doctrine of the Muʿtazilī school of Baghdad. The Basran doctrine became characteristic of Caspian Zaydism and spread from there also to Yaman against the opposition of a local school clinging to the theology of al-Hādī. Al-Muʾayyad also wrote two *fiqh* works based on the legal doctrine of al-Hādī and another one, the *Kitāb al-Ifāda,* in which he elaborated his own views. On its basis he was considered by some the founder of a distinct Zaydī law school, the Muʾayyadiyya, though others counted the Muʾayyadiyya among the Qāsimiyya. Evidently the differences between them were relatively minor.

Ray still remained an important center of Zaydī learning after the fall of the Buwayhids throughout the fifth/eleventh and the first half of the sixth/twelfth century. It was probably there that the Ḥasanid al-Muwaffaq bi llāh Abū ʿAbd Allāh al-Ḥusayn b. Ismāʿīl al-Shajarī al-Jurjānī, a student of Qāḍī ʿAbd al-Jabbār and companion of al-Muʾayyad, taught. He is the author of an extant *Kitāb al-Iḥāṭa* in which he expounded Muʿtazilī theology of the school of ʿAbd al-Jabbār and the Zaydī doctrine of the imamate. His son al-Murshad bi llāh Yaḥyā (d. 477/1084–1085) was a prominent scholar in Ray combining erudition in Muʿtazilī theology, Zaydī law, tradition and genealogy of the Ṭālibids. In 446/1054–1055 he briefly claimed the Zaydī imamate among the Daylamites and was later addressed in Ray as al-Kiyā Yaḥyā

35. *Der Imam al-Qāsim,* pp. 177–181.

and as the imam. Sunnite traditionists also frequented him.[36] The distinguished Muʿtazilī traditionist Ismāʿīl b. ʿAlī al-Sammān (d. ab. 447/1056) in Ray was an expert in Zaydī law as well as in Ḥanafite and Shāfiʿite law. About the middle of the sixth/twelfth century, Abu l-ʿAbbās Aḥmad b. Abi l-Ḥasan al-Kannī was active as a Zaydī scholar and teacher in Ray and in his hometown Kan in the mountains nearby. He is known chiefly as the transmitter of a large number of books by Caspian Zaydī authors to the Yamanite Qāḍī Jaʿfar b. Abī Yaḥyā who studied for some time with him and introduced these works in Yaman.

Another center of Zaydī scholarship in Iran outside the Caspian provinces was Bayhaq. According to Ibn Funduq, the *raʾīs* of Bayhaq Abu l-Qāsim ʿAlī b. Muḥammad b. al-Ḥusayn founded four *madrasas* there some time before Jumādā I 414/July 1023 for four factions: the Ḥanafites, the Shāfiʿites, the Karrāmiyya, and the Sayyids and their followers, Muʿtazilīs (*ʿadliyyūn*) and Zaydīs.[37] The ʿAlids of the town were evidently associated with Zaydism and Muʿtazilī theology. The *raʾīs* was then called to Ghazna by sultan Maḥmūd and reproached, presumably for building a *madrasa* for Shiʿites. Ibn Funduq does not mention whether the *madrasa* was allowed to continue. Later during the century, Abū Saʿd al-Muḥsin b. Muḥammad b. Karāma, known as al-Ḥākim al-Jushamī (d. 494/1101), taught in the region of Bayhaq. Al-Jushamī was a Muʿtazilī Ḥanafite with strong bonds to the Zaydiyya whom he joined in his later life. His numerous works on theology, Qurʾan exegesis, Muʿtazilī and Zaydī apologetics and biography gained considerable authority and popularity among the Caspian Zaydīs and later also in Yaman. His teaching was continued in Bayhaq by his son al-Faḍl among whose students was Abu l-Ḥusayn Zayd b. al-Ḥasan al-Bayhaqī. The latter came to Yaman in 541/1146 and stayed there teaching for two years. The reigning imam al-Mutawakkil ʿala llāh Aḥmad b. Sulaymān studied theology and legal methodology with him and his own works reflect the influence of the Caspian Zaydiyya. Among al-Bayhaqī's other students was the previously mentioned Qāḍī Jaʿfar who accompanied him when he left Yaman. After al-Bayhaqī's death in Tihāma he continued on his way to Iraq and Ray with the mission of gathering the literary heritage of the Zaydīs there and transferring it to Yaman.

Zaydism was now in decline in Iraq and Iran and soon virtually

36. *Der Imam al-Qāsim,* pp. 184–185. Ibn Ḥajar, *Lisān al-mīzān,* VI, p. 247 and VI, pp. 248–249, gives two vitas of him; Ibn al-Jawzī, *al-Muntaẓam,* IX, p. 35; Ibn Ṭabāṭabā, *Muntaqilat al-Ṭālibiyya,* ed. al-Kharsān, p. 156.

37. Ibn Funduq, *Tārīkh-i Bayhaq,* pp. 194–195.

disappeared outside its inaccessible retreats in Rūyān, Daylamān and Gilan. Even there its hold was narrowed by the inroads of Ismaʿilism and Sunnism. Small Zaydī communities survived, however, both of the Nāṣiriyya and the Muʾayyadiyya branch,[38] and maintained a limited tradition of Zaydī learning until the early Safavid age. Under Shāh Ṭahmāsp, ab. 933/1526, most of the remaining Caspian Zaydīs converted to Twelver Shiʿism.

38. *Der Imam al-Qāsim,* p. 218; Shāh Ṭahmāsb Ṣafawī, *Majmūʿa-yi asnād wa mukātabāt-i tārīkhī,* ed. ʿAbd al-Ḥusayn Nawāʾī, pp. 108–109.

Isma^cilism: The Old and the New *Da^cwa*

Among the three major branches of the Shīʿa, the Ismāʿīliyya had the most intimate ties with pre-Mongol Iran. The Ismāʿīlī movement in its historically recognizable form was born in Iran and initially spread from there. At a later stage, Persian Ismaʿilism broke loose from the broader Ismāʿīlī community headed and governed by the Fatimid caliphate of Egypt and formed its own, distinct tradition in the Nizārī movement.

Formally the Ismāʿīliyya was a branch of the Imāmiyya arising from a schism about the succession to imam Jaʿfar al-Ṣādiq. The latter had at first designated his eldest son, Ismāʿīl, as his successor. Ismāʿīl, however, died in the lifetime of his father. The heresiographers mention the existence of at least two, presumably Kufan, Ismāʿīlī groups after the death of Jaʿfar in 148/765 who either denied Ismāʿīl's death and expected his return as the Mahdī or traced the imamate through him to his son Muḥammad b. Ismāʿīl. Nothing is known about the further fate of these early Ismāʿīlī splinter sects if they deserve this description. They must have been numerically insignificant. An Ismāʿīlī movement did not emerge until a century later. There is no definite evidence for any continuous doctrinal tradition linking the early Kufan Ismāʿīlīs and the movement of the second half of the third/ninth century.

This movement was characterized by an intense, secret missionary effort and revolutionary activity. Its elaborate doctrinal system was disseminated by *dāʿīs* throughout the Islamic world. It was centrally directed at first from ʿAskar Mukram and Ahvaz in Khuzistan. From Ahvaz probably came the *dāʿī* ʿAbdān, the first author of Ismāʿīlī doctrinal works, who was active in the region of Kufa as the adviser of the native chief *dāʿī* Ḥamdān Qarmaṭ.[1] When the leader of the movement later moved to Basra and then to Salamiyya in Syria, there is some vague evidence of one branch of his family residing in Ṭāliqān in eastern Iran. Our sources provide a fairly detailed account of the early missionary activity in the countryside of Kufa. From there missionaries were dispatched to Yaman, al-Baḥrayn, and Syria, and the *dāʿī* of Yaman, Ibn Ḥawshab Manṣūr al-Yaman, in turn sent *dāʿīs* who founded the missions in Sind, Egypt, and the Maghrib. Much less information is available about the early Ismāʿīlī missionaries in Iran.[2]

1. "ʿAbdān b. al-Rabīṭ," in *E. Ir.*
2. S. M. Stern, "The Early Ismāʿīlī Missionaries in North-West Persia and in Khurāsān and Transoxania," in *BSOAS*, pp. 56–90.

The *dāʿīs* there, unlike in the Arab countries, were not sent from Iraq and were not dependent on the *daʿwa* there. The exact date of the beginnings of the missionary activity in Iran is unknown but there is reason to assume that it began not later than in Iraq and perhaps slightly earlier. Ismāʿīlī *dāʿīs* soon were active in the region of Ray, Nishapur, and elsewhere in Khurasan, Transoxania and in Fars.

The doctrine spread by the Ismāʿīlī missionaries at this stage essentially comprised a cyclical history of revelation and a gnostic cosmology. Revelation proceeded, according to this doctrine, through seven prophetic eras, each inaugurated by a Speaker (*nāṭiq*) prophet bringing a divine scriptural message. The first six Speakers were Adam, Noah, Abraham, Moses, Jesus, and Muḥammad. Each one was succeeded by a Legatee (*waṣī*), also called a Silent one (*ṣāmit*), who revealed the esoteric truth concealed in the messages. They were Seth, Sem, Ishmael, Aaron, Simon Peter, and ʿAlī. Each cycle was completed by seven imams, the last of whom would rise in rank to become the Speaker of the next cycle and bring a new scripture and law abrogating the previous one. In the sixth era Muḥammad b. Ismāʿīl was the seventh imam, who was thus entitled to become the seventh Speaker. He had disappeared but was about to return in this rank when he would abrogate the law of Islam. His divine message would not entail a new law, however, but would consist in the full revelation of the previously secret esoteric truths. As the eschatological Qāʾim and Mahdī, he would rule and consummate the world.

The basis of this view of history is thoroughly Shiʿite Islamic. The Speakers before Muḥammad and their successors were biblical prophets and figures recognized by the Qurʾan and revered by the Muslims. The expected Mahdī was Muḥammad b. Ismāʿīl, descendant of ʿAlī and Fāṭima. Although he was to abolish the law of Islam, it was merely to reveal fully the truths previously concealed in it and in the scriptures of the earlier prophets. With such a view of the history of true religion, the Nizārī Ismāʿīlī chronicler reporting about the Khurramiyya quoted above could obviously only ridicule their ideas of the divinely ordained imamate having been vested in the Persian kings before Muḥammad and devolving on the Persian Abū Muslim whose grandson, according to their belief, would return as the Mahdī to restore the true Persian religion.

The gnostic cosmology espoused by the early Ismāʿīlī movement was much less Islamic or even Shiʿite, in spite of the presence of some Islamic concepts and terminology.[3] It described the Supreme God as

3. See S. M. Stern, "The Earliest Cosmological Doctrines of Ismāʿīlism," in *Studies in Early Ismāʿīlism,* pp. 3–29; H. Halm, *Kosmologie und Heilslehre der frühen Ismāʿīlīya.*

the Absolute One and as beyond cognition. Through His Intention (*irāda*) and Will (*mashī'a*) he created a light addressing it with the Qur'anic Creative Imperative *kun* consisting of the letters *Kāf* and *Nūn*. From these two letters proceeded through duplication the first, preceding (*sābiq*) principle Kūnī, (the feminine form of *kun*). On the order of God, Kūnī created the second, following (*tālī*) principle, Qadar (ordainment). Kūnī represented the female principle and Qadar the male. Together they comprised seven letters which were called the Seven Higher Letters (*ḥurūf 'ulwiyya*) and were interpreted as the archetypes of the seven Speaker prophets and their scriptures. In the spiritual world Kūnī created seven Cherubs (*karūbiyya*) and Qadar, on Kūnī's order, produced twelve spiritual ranks (*ḥudūd rūḥāniyya*). Another six ranks emanated from Kūnī when she initially failed to recognize the Creator above her. As these six originated without her will through the power of the Creator, she now recognized Him testifying: There is no God but God, and denying her own divinity. Three of these ranks were above her and three below. Among these latter was Iblīs, who refused, when ordered by Kūnī, to submit to Qadar, the heavenly Adam, and thus became the chief satan. Kūnī and Qadar also formed a pentad together with three spiritual forms, Jadd, Fatḥ and Khayāl, which were often identified with the archangels Jibrā'īl, Mīkā'īl, and Isrāfīl, and mediated between the spiritual world and the religious hierarchy in the physical world. The lower, physical world was created by God through the mediation of Kūnī and Qadar.

The gnostic nature of this cosmology is apparent. Many of its structural elements, concepts, and symbolic numbers have parallels in earlier gnostic systems. Yet aside from the Islamic elements like the creative imperative *kun*, the divine attributes of Intention and Will, they cannot be traced to specific sources and models. The assertion of the anti-Ismā'īlī polemicists and heresiographers that Isma'ilism was derived from various dualist religions, Zoroastrianism, Manichaeism, Bardesan, Mazdakism and the Khurramdīniyya is not borne out by its early doctrine. Kūnī and Qadar do not reflect a cosmic dualism of light and darkness, good and evil, but are the first two principles around which the spiritual higher world revolves. The terminology and the names of the various spiritual ranks contain no Persian words or obvious calques on Persian terms.

The early Ismā'īlī movement split about the year 286/899 into two branches.[4] One branch continued to recognize the leadership of 'Abd

4. For the following see in general "Fāṭimiden und Baḥrainqarmaṭen" and "Das Imamat in der frühen ismailitischen Lehre."

Allāh (ʿUbayd Allāh), the future Fatimid caliph al-Mahdī, after he repudiated the expectation of the advent of Muḥammad b. Ismāʿīl and claimed the imamate for himself. The other branch broke with him and generally reaffirmed their belief in the return of Muḥammad b. Ismāʿīl. The latter branch, which for the sake of convenience may be called the Qarmaṭīs (though the historical usage of the name is not so clear-cut) comprised the communities in Iraq, al-Baḥrayn, and most of those in Iran. The Fatimid branch included mainly the Yamanite community founded by Ibn Ḥawshab and those founded by the *dāʿīs* sent by him in the Maghrib, Egypt and Sind. Some of the Ismāʿīlīs in Khurasan, probably a minority, also remained loyal to the Fatimids.

The Qarmaṭis achieved their most spectacular success in al-Baḥrayn where they established their own state. Their leading ideological authorities, however, lived mostly in Iran. Muḥammad b. Aḥmad al-Nasafī (Nakhshabī in Persian), *dāʿī* in Transoxania, wrote a *Kitāb al-Maḥṣūl,* probably about the year 300/911, which found wide acceptance among the Qarmaṭīs as a comprehensive exposition of their esoteric thought. It introduced, apparently for the first time, the Neoplatonic Ismāʿīlī cosmology which largely replaced the earlier doctrine and later was also adopted by Fatimid Ismaʿilism.

In 311/923 the Qarmaṭīs of al-Baḥrayn under the leadership of Abū Ṭāhir, youngest son of the founder of the Qarmaṭī state Abū Saʿīd al-Jannābī, started a series of devastating campaigns into southern Iraq sacking Basra and Kufa and raiding pilgrims' caravans. The Qarmaṭī *dāʿīs* in al-Baḥrayn, Iraq, and Iran were at this time predicting the advent of the Mahdī, Muḥammad b. Ismāʿīl, and the beginning of the seventh, final religious era after the conjunction of Jupiter and Saturn in the year 316/928. The *dāʿī* of Ray, Abū Ḥātim al-Rāzī (d. 322/934), in particular actively spread this prediction. Abū Ḥātim claimed superior authority among the Qarmaṭī *dāʿīs* as the lieutenant (*khalīfa*) of the absent imam and carried on a correspondence with Abū Ṭāhir. He succeeded in converting a number of powerful men in the region of Ray and sent *dāʿīs* throughout northwestern Iran.

The campaigns of Abū Ṭāhir reached their climax in 317/930 with his sacking of Mekka during the pilgrimage season. The Qarmaṭīs committed a barbarous massacre among the pilgrims and inhabitants and carried off the Black Stone of the Kaʿba as a palpable demonstration of the end of the era of Islam. Two years later, in Ramaḍān 319/September–October 931, Abū Ṭāhir surrendered the rule in al-Baḥrayn to a young Persian from Isfahan whom he proclaimed as the expected Mahdī. The date was chosen, according to al-Bīrūnī, to coincide with the passing of 1,500 years from the death of Zoroaster, at the end of the year 1242 of the era of Alexander for which prophecies attributed to Zoroaster and Jāmāsp were predicting the restoration of a the reign of the Magians. The Iṣfahānī Mahdī indeed turned out to be rather a restorer of Persian religion than that descendant of 'Alī and Fāṭima who had been expected by the Ismā'īlīs to reveal the truths concealed in the scriptures of the Prophets of Judaism, Christianity, and Islam. It was claimed that he was a descendant of the Persian kings. His hometown Isfahan had long been associated by the astrologers with the rise of a Persian dynasty which would overthrow the Arab caliphate. He was said to be a Magian and ordered the worship of fire. There were evidently some links with established Zoroastrianism, for the chief priest of the Magians, Isfandiyār b. Adharbād, was accused of complicity with Abū Ṭāhir and executed by the caliph al-Rāḍī.[5] Islamic worship and law were abolished; the Islamic prophets from Abraham to Muḥammad and the imams from 'Alī on were cursed in public. According to a Sunnite eyewitness, Abū Ṭāhir expressly repudiated the teaching of the Ismā'īlī *dā'īs* and told his followers that the true religion which had now been made public was that of "our father Adam." The later prophets, Moses, Jesus, and Muḥammad were all impostors. Al-Nasafī had described the revelation of Adam, in contrast to those of the later prophets, as purely spiritual without a religious law. The reign of the Iṣfahānī Mahdī lasted only eighty days. After he had ordered the death of some prominent Qarmaṭī leaders, Abū Ṭāhir seized and killed him. He now admitted to his followers that he had been duped.

The significance of this episode must be judged with caution. It is evident that the idea of a restoration of Persian religion and Persian reign cannot have been spontaneouslv put forth by the Iṣfāhānī Mahdī. Abū Ṭāhir and some other Qa.maṭī leaders in al-Baḥrayn must have favored, and to some extent planned, it in advance. Abū Sa'īd al-Jannābī was a Persian from Ganāfa, a town on the coast of Fars and was active there as a *dā'ī* before being sent to al-Baḥrayn. Persian sentiments must have remained strong in the family. Among his grandsons at least two bore royal Persian names. Abū Ṭāhir gave one of his sons the name Sābūr (Shapur) and his brother Abu l-Qāsim named one of his Kisrā (Khosrow).

Ismā'īlī doctrine with its syncretistic view of religious history also

5. Al-Mas'ūdī, *al-Tanbīh wa l-ishrāf*, ed. M. J. de Goeje, pp. 104–105.

gave Zoroastrianism and other dualist religions a place in the chain of prophetic revelation. Al-Nasafī had maintained in his *Kitāb al-Maḥṣūl* that the Zoroastrians were followers of the religion of the third Speaker, Abraham.[6] He seems to have claimed that Zoroaster was a missionary appointed by Abraham and was inspired by him when he ordered his followers to turn toward the sun and introduced the practice of tying four knots on their ritual girdles. He also asserted that the Zoroastrians themselves said that Abraham was their prophet and that according to them Adam and Noah were also prophets, Adam being the beginning and Abraham the goal. Mani, Bardesanes, and Marcion were identified by al-Nasafī as leaders of the Sabians and as such they were disciples of the fifth Speaker, Jesus. Al-Nasafī thus seems to have had a positive view of these religions admitting their genuine, if marginal, prophetic origin, though obviously they, like Judaism and Christianity, were superseded by Islam and by the future revelation of the seventh Speaker.

While Abū Ṭāhir thus could perhaps expect a certain amount of sympathy for some aspects of Persian religious tradition among the Ismāʿīlīs, his transformation of the Mahdī into a restorer of Persian religion and kingship required a total repudiation of much of traditional Ismāʿīlī doctrine and expectations concerning the seventh Speaker prophet. The assertion of the Muʿtazilī and anti-Ismāʿīlī polemicist Qāḍī ʿAbd al-Jabbār that Abū Ṭāhir told his followers that his radical turn had been in accordance with "a secret which he and his predecessors had guarded for sixty years" is hardly credible. Rather it was the episode of the Iṣfahānī which gave rise to the persistent charges of the polemicists that at the core of the secret Ismāʿīlī doctrine lay a dualist atheism and that its founders were a group of fanatically anti-Arab Persian Shuʿūbīs plotting to destroy Islam and the reign of the Arabs while hiding in a cloak of Shiʿism.

The quick overthrow of the false Mahdī by Abū Ṭāhir may have been forced upon him as much by widespread hostile reaction among the Ismāʿīlīs as by the outrageous conduct of the Iṣfahānī. There were, in any case, massive defections among the Qarmaṭīs in Iraq and western Iran in the aftermath of the affair. Abū Ḥātim al-Rāzī was forced to flee and hide from his former followers. It was most likely at this stage of his career that he wrote his *Book of Correction, Kitāb al-Iṣlāḥ,* in criticism of some aspects of al-Nasafī's *Kitāb al-Maḥṣūl.* For some of

6. See S. M. Stern, "Abū Ḥātim al-Rāzī on Persian Religion," in *Studies on Early Ismāʿīlism,* pp. 30ff.

the points to which he took exception most vigorously were obviously those which had led the Qarmaṭīs of al-Baḥrayn astray. Thus Abū Ḥātim objected persistently to the antinomian tendencies apparent in some of the teaching of al-Nasafī. Against al-Nasafī he affirmed that both Adam, the first Speaker prophet, and Jesus, the fifth, had brought a religious law. He strongly argued that all esoteric truth inevitably requires an exoteric revealed law. This obviously implied a veiled criticism of Abū Ṭāhir's claim of having restored the lawless religion of Adam.

While Abū Ḥātim could not contradict the Ismā'īlī consensus that the seventh Speaker prophet, Muḥammad b. Ismā'īl, would not bring a law but reveal the spiritual truth of all previous laws, he insisted that the era of Muḥammad had not come to an end with the first presence and disappearance of the seventh imam as implied in al-Nasafī's doctrine. There was, he maintained, an interval or interregnum (*fatra*) between the seventh imam and the advent of the Speaker prophet who would inaugurate the new era. During this interval the religious hierarchy was headed by twelve *lāḥiq*s residing in the twelve provinces (*jazā'ir*) of the earth. One of the twelve was the lieutenant (*khalīfa*) of the absent imam and as such he was entitled to act as the authoritative arbiter among them. There is reason to assume that Abū Ḥātim saw himself in this position. The twelve *lāḥiq*s were, however, all equal in rank, and the *khalīfa* could not control them. The *fatra* thus was a time in which heresies and disputes might arise, even in the hierarchy. An unjust *lāḥiq* might gain control over, and oppress, the hierarchy and falsely claim the rank of the Speaker since the advent of the latter was known to be close. This happened, according to Abū Ḥātim, in the *fatra* of the third era. It may presumably also have happened in the case of al-Mahdī, the founder of the Fatimid caliphate, and perhaps with Abū Ṭāhir, both of whom deceived their followers by premature and false claims of the advent of the seventh Speaker.

Abū Ḥātim also objected to al-Nasafī's views about the Zoroastrians and other dualist religions. He denied that Zoroaster could have been a follower of Abraham. Rather he belonged to the interregnum of the era of the fourth Speaker, Moses. Zoroaster was a *lāḥiq* of the time of David, the *khalīfa* in the absence of the imam, and prescribed to the people of his province various rules and composed a scripture containing wisdom but no religious law. His followers, however, changed his precepts. The position of Zoroastrianism in the fourth era corresponded to that of the Sabians in the fifth. Abū Ḥātim evidently identified the same dualist religions with the Sabians as did al-Nasafī.

The founder of the Sabian religion was a *lāḥiq* and therefore his scripture, called al-Zabūr, contained no laws. Both groups believed in two principles because they misunderstood the statements of the sage who founded their religion. He spoke to them of dualities in order to demonstrate through them the unity of God, but they took his words literally. The adversaries used this false belief to establish their worldly rule.

The rank of the founders of these religions is thus distinctly downgraded. They were not disciples of the Speaker prophets as al-Nasafī had suggested but merely *lāḥiq*s secondary to the *khalīfa* of their time. Their followers, moreover, had misunderstood and changed their teaching. Even more negative was an alternative interpretation of the position of these founders of dualist religions offered by Abū Ḥātim. According to it the Sabians were rather the followers of an adversary who misinterpreted the Christian teaching of the *lāḥiq* of his time. Likewise, Abū Ḥātim adds, Zoroastrianism may have been founded by an adversary who rose up against a *lāḥiq*, presumably David, of the fourth era. In this interpretation no trace of a prophetic origin of Zoroastrianism and the other dualist religions is left.

The efforts of Abū Ḥātim al-Rāzī to restore the ideological unity of Qarmaṭī Isma^cilism and to heal the wound inflicted by the disastrous outcome of the episode of the false Mahdī were not successful. His criticism of al-Nasafī aroused resentment among the Khurasanian and Transoxanian Ismā^cīlīs who continued to consider his *Kitāb al-Maḥṣūl* as authoritative. The eastern *dā^cī* Abū Ya^cqūb al-Sijistānī refuted Abū Ḥātim's *Book of Correction* in his *Book of Support, Kitāb al-Nuṣra,* in which he uncompromisingly upheld most of al-Nasafī's positions. Later Abū Ya^cqūb himself, however, became embroiled in a quarrel with the school of al-Nasafī about the proper method of initiatory instruction. While the latter and his followers held that the teaching should at first primarily deal with the soul, the prophetic cycles, and the problem of creation, Abū Ya^cqūb maintained that the instruction must begin with the *sharī^ca* and its symbolical interpretation (*ta'wīl*).[7] No more is known about this dispute although our source describes it as provoking much enmity between the two sides.

The lack of a united leadership and ideological disagreement evidently aided the Fatimid efforts to regain the allegiance of the dissident Ismā^cīlī communities in the east. The fourth Fatimid caliph, al-Mu^cizz (341–365/953–975), in particular was eager to enlist their sup-

7. Stern, *Studies in Early Ismā^cīlism,* p. 308.

port in his drive eastward to conquer the ʿAbbasid caliphate. Abū Yaʿqūb al-Sijistānī was won over by him and fully backed the Fatimid imamate in his later works. He thus became the chief representative of the Persian school of Ismāʿīlī Neoplatonism in Fatimid Ismaʿilism. A portion of the earlier works of the school also entered Fatimid literature at this time though apparently in a purged form. The school of al-Nasafī in eastern Iran seems to have survived somewhat longer. Gradually, however, all Qarmaṭī communities in Iraq and Iran were absorbed into the Fatimid fold, or disintegrated, probably before the end of the fourth/tenth century. Only the Qarmaṭīs in al-Baḥrayn continued to go their own way until the destruction of their state in 470/1077–1078. Very little is known, however, about their specific religious beliefs.

Persian Ismaʿilism remained tied to the Fatimid caliphate for about a century. It made some notable contributions to Fatimid Ismaʿilism in this period. Three outstanding Persian *dāʿīs* in particular deserve brief mention here. Ḥamīd al-Dīn al-Kirmānī, active in Basra and Baghdad in the time of the caliph al-Ḥākim (386–411/996–1021), propounded a new cosmology evidently influenced by the Muslim philosophers of the school of al-Fārābī. Al-Muʾayyad fi l-Dīn al-Shīrāzī (d. 470/1077), born in Shiraz as the son of an Ismāʿīlī *dāʿī*, converted the Buwayhid amir Abū Kālījār to Ismaʿilism. Later he was forced to flee to Cairo where he was appointed chief *dāʿī* by the Fatimid caliph al-Mustanṣir and wrote numerous doctrinal works and sermons. He and al-Kirmānī became the most influential authors in post-Fatimid Ṭayyibī Ismaʿilism in Yaman and India. Nāṣir-i Khosrow, the Persian poet and traveler, was born near Balkh and was in his later life active as a Fatimid *dāʿī* in Yumgān in the mountains of Badakhshan where he wrote and taught until his death ab. 481/1088. He became the founder and patron saint of the Ismāʿīlī community of Badakhshan which has preserved many of his Ismāʿīlī works. Some of these are Persian translations and adaptations of earlier books in Arabic. Most important is his *Book Joining the Two Wisdoms, Kitāb Jāmiʿ al-ḥikmatayn,* in which he analyzed agreement and disagreement of the views of the Muslim philosophers and of the "prophetic wisdom" of Ismāʿīlī gnosis.

After the death of al-Mustanṣir in 487/1094 the Persian Ismāʿīlīs under the leadership of Ḥasan-i Ṣabbāḥ broke with the Fatimid caliphate and the leadership of the *daʿwa* in Cairo. They recognized the rights of the caliph's disinherited and later murdered son Nizār. The Ismāʿīlī communities dispersed in various regions of Iran had been reorganized under a single leadership already by Ḥasan-i Ṣabbāḥ's teacher and master ᶜAbd al-Malik b. ᶜAṭṭāsh. Ḥasan-i Ṣabbāh, originally probably a Twelver Shiᶜite from Qom, continued Ibn ᶜAṭṭāsh's activity inspiring his followers with a fresh revolutionary vigor. The Ismāᶜīlīs seized and built impregnable mountain strongholds in various parts of the country. In 483/1090 Ḥasan-i Ṣabbāḥ occupied Alamūt northwest of Qazvin which was to remain the headquarters of the Nizārī movement until its surrender to the Mongol conquerors in 654/1256. Ḥasan-i Ṣabbāḥ's grip on the Ismāᶜīlī communities in Iran was impressively demonstrated by the fact that there was no dissent in favor of al-Mustanṣir's successor on the Egyptian throne. Outside Iran some Ismāᶜīlī communities in Syria, especially in the north, joined the Nizārī cause. They recognized from the beginning the leadership of Ḥasan-i Ṣabbāḥ as the representative of the absent imam.

Nizārī Ismāᶜīlism was thus essentially a Persian revolutionary movement rather than a mere schism about the succession to the imamate. Ḥasan-i Ṣabbāh underlined its doctrinal independence by elaborating a new missionary ideology which became known as the "new preaching (*daᶜwa jadīda*)" of Ismaᶜilism. At its core was the thesis of mankind's permanent need for *taᶜlīm,* divinely inspired and authoritative teaching, which was basic to much of Shiᶜite thought in general. Ḥasan-i Ṣabbāḥ developed it in a series of complex logical arguments establishing the inadequacy of human reason in gaining knowledge of God and then went on to demonstrate that only the Ismāᶜīlī imam was such a divinely guided teacher. After this doctrine the Nizārīs came to be commonly called Taᶜlīmīs and Sunnite opponents of Ismaᶜilism like al-Ghazālī concentrated their efforts on refuting it. In itself Ḥasan-i Ṣabbāḥ's teaching was hardly a radical challenge to Islam. Like Fatimid Ismaᶜilism, he insisted on the validity and strict application of the *sharīᶜa.* However, by exalting the autonomous teaching authority of each imam in his time, in independence from his predecessors, Ḥasan-i Ṣabbāḥ paved the way for the great outburst of religious radicalism and antinomianism of the later Alamūt period.

Like Nāṣir-i Khosrow, Ḥasan-i Ṣabbāḥ wrote in Persian, and Persian became the primary language of Nizārī religious literature in the Alamūt period. It was the first time that a major Islamic group adopted Persian instead of Arabic as its religious language. The use of Persian also tended to isolate the Iranian Nizārīs from the Arabic-speaking Ismāᶜīlīs. Important Persian religious texts must have been translated into Arabic for the Syrian Nizārīs, yet there is little evidence that they had much impact there. Syrian Nizārī religious literature developed largely independently of the Persian literature even during the Alamūt period. The Arabic Fatimid literature seems to have preserved a much greater influence there than in Iran.

On the political plane, Ḥasan-i Ṣabbāḥ initiated a policy of armed revolt against the Saljūq sultanate backed by the Sunnite establishment. The Nizārīs captured numerous mountain fortresses in the Elburz range, fortified towns in Quhistān in northwestern Iran and later also mountain strongholds in northern Syria. In confrontation with the overwhelming military power of the Saljūq opponents, Ḥasan-i Ṣabbāḥ introduced the policy of spectacular assassination of prominent leaders, military and religious, by *fidāʾīs*, self-sacrificing devotees, for the purpose of intimidation. Their conduct seemed so irrational to the opponents that they called them hashish addicts, *ḥashīshiyyūn*.[8] Their sanguinary practice could not fail to raise the long-standing extreme antagonism between Ismāʿīlīs and other Muslims, Sunnite and Shiʿite alike, to a still higher pitch.

The Nizārī defiance of established Islam reached its climax in the proclamation of the Resurrection (*qiyāma*) by Ḥasan ʿalā dhikrihi l-salām on 17 Ramaḍān 559/8 August 1164. The *sharīʿa*, symbol of the reign of Islam, was formally abrogated. The resurrection was interpreted as the manifestation of the unveiled Truth in the spiritual reality of the imam which actualized Paradise for the faithful capable of grasping it while condemning the opponents who continued to adhere to the shell of the law to the Hell of spiritual nonbeing. The *qiyāma* in substance repeated the proclamation of the advent of the Mahdī and the end of the era of Islam by the Qarmaṭīs of al-Baḥrayn two centuries before. It did so, however, without the Persian trappings of the earlier episode, without the restoration of fire worship and Persian kingship.

The momentum of the *qiyāma* could not permanently be sustained. Half a century later Ḥasan's grandson, Jalāl al-Dīn Ḥasan, repudiated the *qiyāma* doctrine and announced his adherence to Sunnite Islam. He publicly cursed his predecessors as infidels, made peace with the ʿAbbasid caliph al-Nāṣir recognizing his suzerainty and ordered his followers to conform to the *sharīʿa* in its Shāfiʿite form. Thus he became commonly known as the New-Muslim (*naw-Musulmān*).

Under Jalāl al-Dīn's son ʿAlāʾ al-Dīn Muḥammad (618–653/1221–

8. The abusive name *ḥashīshī* occurs in Caspian Zaydī texts applied to the Nizārīs of Alamūt and the Elburz mountains (see *Arabic Texts Concerning the History of the Zaydī Imāms of Ṭabaristān, Daylamān and Gīlān*, pp. 146, 329). The assumption that the term was local to Syria and was never used in Persia (B. Lewis, "Ḥashīshiyya" in *E.I.*, 2nd ed.) is thus erroneous.

1255) the application of the *sharīʿa* was again relaxed though not formally abolished. In this last phase of the Alamūt period, Nizārī Ismaʿilism was still intellectually attractive enough to gain the adherence of a philosopher of the stature of Naṣīr al-Dīn Ṭūsi, a native Twelver Shiʿite.[9] In a spiritual autobiography written in the time of his Ismāʿīlī allegiance, Ṭūsī described his upbringing as a strict adherent of the *sharīʿa* and his subsequent study of scholastic theology (*kalām*) and philosophy. While he found philosophy most satisfactory, he discovered that its principles were shaky when the discourse reached its ultimate goal, the knowledge of God and the origins and destiny of man. He recognized the need of reason for an infallible teacher to guide it toward its perfection. His conversion to Nizārī Ismaʿilism was, he indicated, facilitated by his acquaintance with the esoteric thought of Tāj al-Dīn al-Shahrastānī, the Sunnite Ashʿarī theologian and student of religions, who a century earlier had likewise secretly been attracted to Nizārī Ismaʿilism.

Ṭūsī thus joined the Nizārīs as a philosopher. In his *Nasirean Ethics* he found no difficulty in identifying the Ismāʿīlī prophets and imams with the philosopher kings, the rulers of the Virtuous City and the Regulators (*mudabbir*) of the world in the Platonic thought of al-Fārābī. As such the imams were the controllers and administrators of the Religious Law which they legislated with divine assistance and applied in accordance with the specific requirements of their time. These ideas were further elaborated by him in his Ismāʿīlī writings. The contradictions in the conduct of the imams, he affirmed, were merely in appearance, since in their spiritual reality they were identical and all acted in accordance with the requirements of their own time. In the era of Muḥammad times of concealment, when the esoteric truth was hidden under the cover of the law, and of resurrection, when it was openly apparent and the law was in abeyance, might alternate in conformity with the autonomous decision of the imam of each time.

Such ideas constituted a radical challenge to established Islam. Yet they were in a broader sense genuinely Islamic. Muslim theologians and jurists of the establishment like al-Ghazālī might well dispute that Muslim philosophers like al-Fārābī and Avicenna were truly Muslims. But these philosophers and the Nizārīs had no doubt that they were Muslims if perhaps more than only Muslims. The radicalism of the ideological challenge of the Nizārīs reflected the radicalism of their

9. For the following see in general "Naṣīr al-Dīn al-Ṭūsī's Ethics between Philosophy, Shiʿism, and Sufism."

political opposition, their essentially revolutionary motivation. In this respect they were the true successors of Mazdakism before Islam and the Khurramiyya in the early ᶜAbbasid age. Niẓām al-Mulk understood this well when he described the continuity between Mazdak, the Khurramiyya, and the Ismāᶜīlīs primarily in terms of their subversive activity, their threat to the order of the state.[10] The Nizārī movement represented Iranian opposition to Saljūq Turkish rule as the Khurramī movement had represented the opposition to ᶜAbbasid Arab domination. Yet while the Khurramiyya opposition hoped for a restoration of Persian religion, the Nizārī opposition was carried on in the name of the hidden, true meaning of Islam. Five centuries after the introduction of Islam in Iran, religious opposition was no longer conceivable in other than Islamic terms.

10. Niẓām al-Mulk, *Siyāsat-nāma,* ed. H. Darke, pp. 254ff.

Bibliography

ʿAbd Allāh b. ʿUmar b. Muḥammad b. Dāwūd Wāʿiẓ-i Balkhī. *Faḍāʾil Balkh,* Persian translation by ʿAbd Allāh Ḥusaynī Balkhī, ed. ʿAbd al-Ḥayy Ḥabībī. Tehran, 1350/1971.

ʿAbd al-Jabbār. *Faḍl al-iʿtizāl wa-ṭabaqāt al-Muʿtazila,* ed. F. Sayyid. Tunis, 1393/1974.

ʿAbd al-Qāhir al-Baghdādī. *K. al-Milal wa l-niḥal,* ed. A. N. Nader. Beirut, 1970.

———. *K. al-Farq bayn al-firaq,* ed. Muḥammad Badr. Cairo, 1910.

Abu l-Faraj al-Iṣfahānī. *K. al-Aghānī.* Bulāq, 1285/1868.

Abū Ghānim Bishr b. Ghānim al-Khurāsānī. *K. al-Mudawwana al-kubrā.* Beirut, 1974.

al-Ashʿarī. *K. Maqālāt al-islāmiyyīn wa-khtilāf al-muṣallīn,* ed. H. Ritter. Istanbul, 1929–1933.

Bahār, Muḥammad Taqī Malik al-Shuʿarāʾ. *Sabk-shināsī,* I. Tehran, 1321/1942.

al-Balādhurī. *Futūḥ al-buldān,* ed. M. J. de Goeje. Leiden, 1866.

———. *Ansāb al-ashrāf,* in W. Ahlwardt, *Anonyme arabische Chronik.* Greifswald, 1883.

Bosworth, C. E. "Notes on the Pre-Ghaznawid History of Eastern Afghanistan," *Islamic Quarterly* IX (1965), pp. 12–24.

———. *Sīstān under the Arabs, from the Islamic Conquest to the Rise of the Ṣaffārids (30–250/651–864).* Rome, 1968.

———. "The Armies of the Ṣaffārids," *Bulletin of the School of Oriental and African Studies,* XXXI (1968), pp. 534–554.

Bulliet, R. W. *The Patricians of Nishapur.* Cambridge, Mass., 1972.

The Cambridge History of Iran. Vol. III, ed. E. Yarshater. Cambridge, 1983.

———. Vol. IV, ed. R. N. Frye. Cambridge, 1975.

Chabbi, J. "Remarques sur le développement historique des mouvements ascétiques et mystiques au Khurasan," *Studia Islamica* XLVI (1977), pp. 5–72.

Christensen, A. *Le Règne du roi Kawādh I et le communisme mazdakite.* Copenhagen, 1925.

al-Dhahabī. *Siyar al-nubalāʾ.* Beirut, 1981–1985.

al-Dīnawarī. *Al-Akhbār al-ṭiwāl,* ed. E. Guirgass. Leiden, 1888.

Encyclopaedia Iranica. Ed. E. Yarshater. London, 1982–.

The Encyclopaedia of Islam. 2nd ed. Leiden, 1960–.

al-Ghujduwānī. *Risāla-yi Ṣāḥibiyya,* ed. S. Nafīsī, in *Farhang-i Īrān Zamīn* I/1, pp. 70–101.
al-Ḥakīm al-Samarqandī. *Al-Sawād al-aʿẓam.* Istanbul, 1304/1887. Persian translation, *Tarjuma-yi sawād al-aʿẓam,* ed. ʿAbd al-Ḥayy Ḥabībī. Tehran, 1348/1969.
Halm, H. *Die Ausbreitung der šāfiʿitischen Rechtsschule von den Anfängen bis zum 8./14. Jahrhundert.* Wiesbaden, 1974.
———. *Kosmologie und Heilslehre der frühen Ismāʿīlīya.* Wiesbaden, 1978.
———. "Das 'Buch der Schatten': Die Mufaḍḍal-Tradition der Ġulāt und die Ursprünge des Nuṣairiertums," *Der Islam* LV (1978), pp. 219–266; LVIII (1981), pp. 15–86.
Hodgson, M. G. S. *The Order of Assassins.* The Hague, 1955.
Hujwiri. *The Kashf al-Mahjūb: The Oldest Persian Treatise on Sufism* by ʿAlī b. ʿUthmān al-Gullābī al-Hujwīrī, trans. R. A. Nicholson. London, 1936.
Ibn Abī Yaʿlā. *Ṭabaqāt al-Ḥanābila,* ed. Muḥammad Ḥāmid al-Fiqī. Cairo, 1962.
Ibn al-Athīr. *K. al-Kāmil fi l-taʾrīkh,* ed. C. J. Tornberg. Leiden, 1851–1876.
Ibn Funduq al-Bayhaqī. *Tārīkh-i Bayhaq,* ed. A. Bahmanyār. Tehran, 1317/1938.
Ibn Ḥajar al-ʿAsqalānī. *Tahdhīb al-tahdhīb.* Hyderabad, 1325–27/1907–1909.
Ibn Ḥawqal. *K. Ṣūrat al-arḍ,* ed. J. H. Kramers. Leiden, 1938–1939.
Ibn al-Jawzī. *Al-Muntaẓam fī taʾrīkh al-mulūk wa l-umam.* Hyderabad, 1357–1362/1938–1943.
———. *Ṣifat al-ṣafwa.* Hyderabad, 1356/1937.
Ibn Khallikān. *Wafayāt al-aʿyān wa-anbāʾ abnāʾ al-zamān,* ed. Iḥsān ʿAbbās. Beirut, 1968–1972.
Ibn-i Munawwar. *Asrār al-Tawḥīd fī maqāmāt al-Shaykh Abī Saʿīd,* ed. Dhabīḥullāh Ṣafā. Tehran, 1332/1953.
Ibn al-Murtaḍā. *Ṭabaqāt al-Muʿtazila,* ed. S. Diwald-Wilzer. Wiesbaden, 1961.
Ibn Muṭahhar al-Ḥillī. *Rijāl al-ʿAllāma al-Ḥillī (Khulāṣat al-aqwāl fī maʿrifat al-rijāl),* ed. Muḥammad Ṣādiq Āl Baḥr al-ʿUlūm. Najaf, 1381/1961.
Ibn al-Nadīm. *K. al-Fihrist,* ed. G. Flügel. Leipzig, 1871.
Ibn al-Qifṭī. *Inbāh al-ruwāt ʿalā anbāh al-nuḥāt,* ed. Muḥammad Abu l-Faḍl Ibrāhīm. Cairo, 1950–1973.
Ibn Rusta. *Al-Aʿlāq al-Nafīsa,* ed. M. J. de Goeje. Leiden, 1892.
Ibn Saʿd. *K. al-Ṭabaqāt al-kabīr,* ed. E. Sachau et al. Leiden, 1905–1940.

Ibn Sallām al-Ibāḍī. *K. Badʾ al-Islām wa-sharāʾiʿ al-dīn,* ed. W. Schwartz and al-Shaykh Sālim b. Yaʿqūb. Wiesbaden, 1986.
Ibn Ṭabāṭabā. *Muntaqilat al-Ṭālibiyya,* ed. Muḥammad Mahdī al-Sayyid Ḥasan al-Kharsān. Najaf, 1381/1960.
Ibn Taymiyya. *Majmūʿat al-rasāʾil wa l-masāʾil,* ed. Muḥammad Rashīd Riḍā. Cairo, 1349/1930.
al-Iṣṭakhrī. *Al-Masālik wa l-mamālik,* ed. M. J. de Goeje. Leiden, 1870.
Jāmī. *Nafaḥāt al-uns min ḥaḍarāt al-quds,* ed. Mahdī Tawḥīdīpūr. Tehran, 1336/1957.
Kāshānī, Abu l-Qāsim. *Tārīkh-i Ismāʿīliyya* (from his *Zubdat al-tawārīkh*), ed. M. T. Dānishpazhūh. Tabriz, 1343/1964.
Kern, F. "Ein dogmatisches Vermächtnis des Imam aš-Šāfiʿī," *Mitteilungen des Seminars für orientalische Sprachen* XIII (1910), pp. 141–145.
Khalīfa b. al-Khayyāṭ. *Taʾrīkh,* ed. Akram Ḍiyāʾ al-ʿUmarī. Beirut, 1397/1977.
al-Khaṭīb al-Baghdādī. *Taʾrīkh Baghdād.* Cairo, 1931.
Klíma, O. *Mazdak: Geschichte einer sozialen Bewegung im sasanidischen Persien.* Prague, 1957.
Kohlberg, E. "Muwāfāt Doctrines in Muslim Theology," *Studia Islamica* LVII (1983), pp. 47–66.
al-Kulaynī. *al-Uṣūl min al-Kāfī,* ed. ʿAlī Akbar al-Ghaffārī, 3rd ed. Tehran, 1388/1968.
Laoust, H. *Essai sur les doctrines sociales et politiques de Takī-d-dīn Aḥmad b. Taimīya canoniste Ḥanbalite.* Cairo, 1939.
Le Strange, G. *The Lands of the Eastern Caliphate,* 2nd ed. Cambridge, 1930.
Madelung, W. "Fatimiden und Baḥrainqarmaṭen," *Der Islam* XXXIV (1959), pp. 34–88.
———. "Das Imamat in der frühen ismailitischen Lehre," *Der Islam* XXXVII (1961), pp. 43–135.
———. *Der Imam al-Qāsim ibn Ibrāhīm und die Glaubenslehre der Zaiditen.* Berlin, 1965.
———. "Abū Isḥāq al-Ṣābī on the Alids of Ṭabaristān and Gīlān," *Journal of Near Eastern Studies* XXVI (1967), pp. 15–57.
———. "Imāmism and Muʿtazilite Theology," in *Le Shîʿisme imâmite,* ed. T. Fahd. Paris, 1970, pp. 13–29.
———. "The Spread of Māturīdism and the Turks," in *Actas do IV Congresso de Estudios Árabes e Islâmicos, Coimbra-Lisboa 1968.* Leiden, 1971, pp. 109–168.
———. "The Origins of the Controversy Concerning the Creation of

the Koran," in *Orientalia Hispanica sive studia F. M. Pareja octogenario dicata,* ed. J. M. Barral, I/1. Leiden, 1974, pp. 504–525.

———. "The Sources of Ismāʿīlī Law," *Journal of Near Eastern Studies* XXXV (1976), pp. 29–40.

———. "Frühe muʿtazilitische Häresiographie: das *Kitāb al-Uṣūl* des Ǧaʿfar b. Ḥarb?" *Der Islam* LVII (1980), pp. 220–236.

———. "Abū ʿĪsā al-Warrāq über die Bardesaniten, Marcioniten und Kantäer," in *Studien zur Geschichte und Kultur des Vorderen Orients: Festschrift für Bertold Spuler zum siebzigsten Geburtstag,* ed. H. R. Roemer and A. Noth. Leiden, 1981.

———. "The Early Murjiʾa in Khurāsān and Transoxania and the Spread of Ḥanafism," *Der Islam* LIX (1982), pp. 32–39.

———. "Naṣīr al-Dīn al-Ṭūsī's Ethics between Philosophy, Shiʿism, and Sufism," in *Ethics in Islam,* ed. R. G. Hovannisian. Malibu, 1985, pp. 85–101.

———. "The Theology of al-Zamakhsharī," in *Actas del XII Congresso de la U.E.A.I. (Málaga, 1984).* Madrid, 1986, pp. 485–495.

———. *Arabic Texts Concerning the History of the Zaydī Imāms of Ṭabaristān, Daylamān and Gīlān.* Beirut, 1987.

al-Malaṭī. *K. al-tanbīh wa l-radd ʿalā ahl al-ahwāʾ wa l-bidaʿ,* ed. S. Dedering. Leipzig, 1936.

al-Maqdisī. *Aḥsan al-taqāsim fī maʿrifat al-aqālīm,* ed. M. J. de Goeje. Leiden, 1906.

al-Masʿūdī. *Murūj al-dhahab,* ed. Barbier de Meynard and Pavet de Courteille, corr. by C. Pellat. Beirut, 1966–1979.

———. *al-Tanbīh wa l-ishrāf,* ed. M. J. de Goeje. Leiden, 1894.

Meier, F. *Die Vita des Scheich Abū Isḥāq al-Kāzarūnī in der persischen Bearbeitung von Maḥmūd b. ʿUṯmān.* Leipzig, 1948.

———. *Die Fawāʾiḥ al-ǧamāl wa-fawātiḥ al-ǧalāl des Naǧm ad-dīn al-Kubrā: Eine Darstellung mystischer Erfahrungen im Islam aus der Zeit um 1200 n. Chr.* Wiesbaden, 1957.

———. *Abū Saʿīd-i Abū l-Ḫayr: Wirklichkeit und Legende.* Tehran-Liège, 1976.

Mélikoff, I. *Le "port-hache" du Khorasan dans la tradition épique turco-iranienne.* Paris, 1962.

Miles, G. C. "Some Arab-Sasanian and Related Coins," *American Numismatic Society Museum Notes* VII (1957), pp. 187–209.

———. "Some New Light on the History of Kirman in the First Century of the Hijrah," in *The World of Islam: Studies in Honour of Philip K. Hitti,* ed. J. Kritzeck and R. B. Winder. London, 1960, pp. 85–98.

Minorsky, V. *Studies on Caucasian History*. London, 1953.
Molé, M. "Les Kubrawiyya entre sunnisme et chiisme au huitième et neuvième siècles de l'hégire," *Revue des Etudes Islamiques* XXVIII (1960), pp. 61–142.
al-Mubarrad. *Al-Kāmil,* ed. W. Wright. Leipzig, 1864–1892.
al-Mufīd. *ʿIddat rasāʾil li l-shaykh . . . Muḥammad b. Muḥammad b. al-Nuʿmān al-ʿUkbarī al-Baghdādī al-mulaqqab bi l-shaykh al-Mufīd*. Qom, n.d.
al-Najāshī. *Al-Rijāl*. Tehran, n.d.
al-Nāshiʾ. *Masāʾil al-imāma,* ed. J. van Ess in *Frühe muʿtazilitische Häresiographie: Zwei Werke des Nāšiʾ al-akbar*. Beirut, 1971.
Nashwān al-Ḥimyarī. *al-Ḥūr al-ʿīn,* ed. Kamāl Muṣṭafā. Cairo, 1367/1948.
al-Nawbakhtī. *K. Firaq al-shīʿa,* ed. H. Ritter. Istanbul, 1931.
Niẓām al-Mulk. *Siyāsat-nāma,* ed. H. Darke. Tehran, 1968.
Pognon, H. *Inscriptions Mandaïtes des Coupes de Khouabir*. Paris, 1898–1899.
Qummī, Ḥasan b. Muḥammad b. Ḥasan. *Tārīkh-i Qum,* ed. Jalāl al-Dīn Tihrānī. Tehran, 1313/1935.
Rashīd al-Dīn. *Jāmiʿ al-tawārīkh: qismat-i Ismāʿīliyya,* ed. M. T. Dānish-pazhūh and M. Mudarrisī. Tehran, 1960.
Ribera y Taragon, J. *Disertaciones y opúsculos*. Madrid, 1928.
Saʿd b. ʿAbd Allāh b. Abī Khalaf al-Qummī. *K. al-Maqālāt wa l-firaq,* ed. M. J. Mashkūr. Tehran, 1963.
al-Ṣafadī. *Al-Wāfī bi l-wafayāt,* vol. VII, ed. Iḥsān ʿAbbās. Wiesbaden, 1969.
al-Samʿānī. *Al-Ansāb,* facs. ed. D. S. Margoliouth. Leiden, 1912.
———. *Al-Taḥbīr fi l-muʿjam al-kabīr,* ed. Munīra Nājī Sālim. Baghdad, 1395/1975.
Schacht, J. "An Early Murciʾite Treatise: The Kitāb al-ʿĀlim wal-Mutaʿallim," *Oriens* XVII (1964), pp. 96–117.
Schaeder, H. H. "Die Kantäer," *Welt des Orients* I (1947–1952), pp. 288–298.
al-Shahrastānī. *K. al-Milal wa l-niḥal,* ed. W. Cureton. London, 1846.
Shāh Ṭahmāsb Ṣafawī. *Majmūʿa-yi asnād wa-mukātabāt-i tārīkhī,* ed. ʿAbd al-Ḥusayn Nawāʾī. Tehran, 1350/1971.
al-Shammākhī. *Al-Siyar*. Cairo, 1301/1884.
Sharon, M. *Black Banners from the East: The Establishment of the ʿAbbāsid State—Incubation of a Revolt*. Jerusalem-Leiden, 1983.
Składanek, B. "The Khārijites in Iran," *Rocznik Orientalistyczny* XLIV/1 (1985), pp. 65–92; XLIV/2 (1985), pp. 89–101.

Stern, S. M. "The Early Missionaries in North-West Persia and in Khurāsān and Transoxania," *Bulletin of the School of Oriental and African Studies* XXIII (1960), pp. 56–90.

———. *Studies in Early Ismaᶜilism.* Jerusalem, 1983.

Strothmann, R. *Das Staatsrecht der Zaiditen.* Strassburg, 1912.

al-Ṭabarī. *Ta'rīkh al-rusul wa l-mulūk,* ed. M. J. de Goeje et al. Leiden, 1879/1901.

al-Ṭūsī. *K. Fihrist kutub al-shīᶜa,* ed. A. Sprenger et al. Calcutta, 1853–1854.

———. *Rijāl al-Ṭūsī,* ed. Muḥammad Ṣādiq Āl Baḥr al-ᶜUlūm. Najaf, 1381/1961.

van Ess, J. "Ḍirār b. ᶜAmr und die 'Cahmīya': Biographie einer vergessenen Schule," *Der Islam* XLIII (1967), pp. 241–279; XLIV (1968), pp. 1–70.

———. "Untersuchungen zu einigen ibāḍitischen Handschriften," *Zeitschrift der Deutschen Morgenländischen Gesellschaft* CXXVI (1976), pp. 25–63.

———. *Ungenutzte Texte zur Karrāmīya: Eine Materialsammlung.* Heidelberg, 1980.

———. "Yazīd b. Unaisa und Abū ᶜĪsā al-Iṣfahānī: Zur Konvergenz zweier sektiererischer Bewegungen," in *Studi in onore di Francesco Gabrieli nel suo ottantesimo compleanno,* ed. R. Traini. Rome, 1984, pp. 301–313.

Walker, J. *A Catalogue of the Muhammadan Coins in the British Museum,* I, *A Catalogue of the Arab-Sassanian Coins.* London, 1941.

Watt, W. M. "Khārijite Thought in the Umayyad Period," *Der Islam,* XXXVI (1960), pp. 215–231.

Wellhausen, J. *Die religiös-politischen Oppositionsparteien im alten Islam.* Berlin, 1901.

———. *Das arabische Reich und sein Sturz.* Berlin, 1902.

Wilkinson, J. C. "The Early Development of the Ibāḍī Movement in Baṣra," in *Studies on the First Century of Islamic Society,* ed. G. H. A. Juynboll. Carbondale, 1982, pp. 125–144.

al-Yaᶜqūbī. *Ta'rīkh,* ed. M. Th. Houtsma. Leiden, 1883.

Yāqūt. *Muᶜjam al-buldān,* ed. F. Wüstenfeld. Leipzig, 1866–1873.

Anon. *Akhbār al-dawla al-ᶜAbbāsiyya,* ed. A. al-Dūrī and A. al-Muṭṭalibī. Beirut, 1971.

———. *Ḥudūd al-ᶜĀlam, The Regions of the World,* trans. V. Minorsky. London, 1937.

———. *Tārīkh-i Sīstān,* ed. Malik al-Shuᶜarā' Bahār. Tehran, 1314/1935.

Index

Aaron, 94
Ābah, 84
ʿAbbasid revolution: Iranian nature of, 8; origins in the Kaysāniyya, 7
ʿAbd Allāh al-Afṭaḥ, 80
ʿAbd Allāh al-Aḥwaṣ, 79
ʿAbd Allāh Barzishābādī, 53
ʿAbd Allāh al-Jūnī (?), 50 and n. 37
ʿAbd Allāh al-Sadīwarī(?), 68
ʿAbd Allāh b. Ghunaym al-Najāshī, 84 n. 24
ʿAbd Allāh b. al-Ḥarb, 7; *see also* cyclical return
ʿAbd Allāh b. al-Ḥārith, *see* ʿAbd Allāh b. al-Ḥarb
ʿAbd Allāh b. Muʿāwiya, 7, 62
ʿAbd Allāh b. Mubārak, 21
ʿAbd Allāh b. Muḥammad b. al-Ḥusayn al-Ahwāzī, 84 n. 24
ʿAbd Allāh b. ʿUmar, 24
ʿAbd Allāh b. Yaḥyā Ṭālib al-Ḥaqq, 73
ʿAbd al-ʿAẓīm al-Ḥasanī, Sayyid, 84
ʿAbd al-ʿAzīz Bishkast, 73–4
ʿAbd al-ʿAzīz b. Abi l'Qāsim Maḥmashādh, 44 n. 23
ʿAbd al-Jabbār al-Hamadhānī, Qāḍī, 30, 90, 98
ʿAbd al-Jabbār al-Khuwārazmī, 38
ʿAbd al-Jalīl al-Rāzī, 35
ʿAbd al-Karīm b. ʿAjarrad, 58 and n. 20, 59–60, 59 n. 23, 60, 62–3, 64 n. 46, 65
ʿAbd al-Khāliq b. ʿAbd al-Jamīl al-Ghujduwānī, 50, 51
ʿAbd al-Malik b. ʿAṭṭāsh, 102
ʿAbd al-Qāhir al-Baghdādī, 58 n. 19, 59 nn. 23 and 24, 60, 63, 64, 65 n. 49, 66 and n. 66, 66–7
ʿAbd Rabbih al-Kabīr, 58 n. 19
ʿAbd Rabbih al-Ṣaghīr, 58 and n. 19
ʿAbd al-Raḥmān, son of Saʿd b. Mālik b. ʿĀmir al-Ashʿarī, 79
ʿAbd al-Raḥmān b. al-Ashʿath: rebellion of, 14, 73, 79
ʿAbd al-Raḥmān b. Rustam, 73, 75
ʿAbd al-Raḥmān b. Samura, 57
ʿAbd al-Raḥmān b. Ziyād. *See* Abū Khālid Ziyād b. ʿAbd al-Raḥmān al-Shaybānī
ʿAbd al-Wahhāb b. ʿAbd al-Raḥmān, 74
ʿAbdalī (*nisba* used for adherents of the school of Ibn Karrām), 44 n. 23
ʿAbdān, 93
Abīward, 60
ablution of the feet, 88–9
Abr Shahr. *See* Nishapur
Abraham, 94, 98, 99
Abu l-ʿAbbās al-Ḥasanī, 90
Abu l-ʿAbbās al-Qāsim al-Sayyārī, 47–8
Abu l-ʿAbbās Aḥmad b. Abi l-Ḥasan al-Kannī, 91
Abu l-ʿAbbās b. Surayj, 26, 28
Abū ʿAbd Allāh al-Baṣrī, 29, 90
Abū ʿAbd Allāh al-Dāmaghānī, 33
Abū ʿAbd Allāh al-Mahdī, 89, 90
Abū ʿAbd Allāh al-Ṣaymarī, 29
Abū ʿAbd Allāh Muḥammad b. Karrām, 39; conversion by, 44; death of, 45; legal doctrine of, 40, 41; theology of, 42–3. *See also* asceticism; *ḥawādith*
Abu l-ʿAlāʾ, son of Dehkhodā Kaykhosrow, 10
Abū ʿAlī, revolt of, 56
Abū ʿAlī al-Manīʿī, 33–4
Abū ʿAlī al-Fārmadhī, 50
Abū ʿAlī Muḥammad b. ʿIsā, 81
Abū ʿAlī b. Junayd, 84

Amol, 27, 85, 88, 89, 90
Anatolia, 48, 49, 50, 51
animals, slaughter of: among the Ṣiyāmiyya, 4
anthropomorphism. See *tashbīh*
apostasy: in doctrine of Jaʿfar al-Ṣādiq, 78
Arab national interest, 13
Arabization: and conversion to Islam, 13
ʿaraḍ (accident), 42
arḍ al-shirk (territory of polytheism), 19, 31
arḍ al-turk (territory of the Turks = *arḍ al-shirk*), 19, 31
Ardabīl, 71
Armenia, 26, 71
asceticism: of Abū Isḥāq al-Kāzarūnī, 48; of Ibn Karrām, 43–4; in practice of the Khurramiyya, 5; in practice of the Māhāniyya, 6; in practice of the Ṣiyāmiyya, 4
Aṣḥāb al-suʾāl, 59 n. 23
Ashʿar, tribe of Ashāʿīra, 78, 80, 81, 82
al-Ashʿarī, 30—31, 59 n. 26, 64 n. 46, 65 n. 49; cursing of, 33, 35
Ashʿarīs, persecution of, 33–4
Ashʿarism, 28–9, 38, 42, 45
Ashʿath b. Isḥāq b. Saʿd, 79
Ashras b. ʿAbd Allāh, 16
Asia, Central, 51, 52
ʿAskar Mukram, 29, 93
aṣlaḥ (best interest), 41
Aspuzār. *See* Isfizār
assassination: policy of Ḥasan-i Ṣabbāḥ, 103
Astarabyān, 70
astrology: in Ismāʿīlī doctrine, 96–7
ʿAṭawiyya, 56, 57
ʿAṭiyya al-Jūzjānī, 60
ʿAṭiyya b. al-Aswad al-Ḥanafī, 57 and n. 14, 58
Aṭrāfiyya, 68 and n. 66
attributes, divine, 67; in doctrine of eastern Ḥanafites, 42; in doctrine of Karrāmiyya, 42–3; in Muʿtazilite doctrine, 41–2; in doctrine of Najjāriyya, 29; *see also* temporality, creation
Avicenna, 104
Azāriqa, 56–7, 58 n. 19, 63 n. 40, 70, 71

Bābak, parentage of, 9
Badakhshan, 101
Bādhghīs, 50
Baghdad, ix, 21, 22, 23, 24, 29, 33, 34–5, 38, 49, 51, 80, 82, 84, 90, 101
Bahāʾ al-Dīn al-Naqshbandī, 51
al-Baḥrayn, 93, 96, 97, 99, 101, 103
Bājarwān, 71
Balāsāghūn, 31
balkafa ('acceptance without questioning the how'), 41
Balkh, 17, 18, 20, 58, 85, 101
Bāmayīn, 50
Bamm, 69
Banū Faḍḍāl, 80
Banū Ḥanīfa, 57
Banu l-Ḥārith b. Kaʿb, 56
Banū Saʿd b. Mālik, 79
Banū Sadūs, 60
Banū Samāʿa, 80
Banū Tamīm, 73
Banū Taym Allāh, 80
al-Bāqillānī, 28
Bar Konai, Theodore, 3, 4, 5, 6 n. 18
barāʾa (dissociation): and the Akhnasiyya, 61; in Khārijite doctrine, 55, 59 n. 25; according to Ziyād b. al-Aṣfar, 71 n. 89
Bardesanes, 95, 98
Barmakids, 4, 87
Barqarūd, 81
Basra, ix, 29, 56, 73, 74, 75, 93, 96, 101

Ibn Ḥanbal. *See* Aḥmad b. Ḥanbal
Ibn Ḥawshab Manṣūr al-Yaman, 93, 96
Ibn Karrām. *See* Abū ʿAbd Allāh Muḥammad b. Karrām.
Ibn Khaldūn, 38
Ibn Khuzayma, 27
Ibn al-Kirmānī, 60
Ibn Mākūlā, 33
Ibn-i Munawwar, 46
Ibn al-Nadīm, 88
Ibn al-Rammāḥ, 20
Ibn Saʿd, 21, 79
Ibn Shādhlūya. *See* Ibrāhīm b. Shādhlūya
Ibn Surayj. *See* Abu l-ʿAbbās b. Surayj
Ibn Taymiyya, 43 and n. 16
Ibrāhīm b. al-Akhḍar, 69
Ibrāhīm b. Muḥammad, 11
Ibrāhīm b. Samāʿa, 80
Ibrāhīm b. Shādhlūya, 71, 72
ijmāʿ, 83
Īlāq, 26
ʿImād al-Dīn al-Iṣfahānī, 36
imamate: in doctrine of Ḥamza b. Ādharak, 66; in Ismāʿīlī doctrine, 94; differing views of Ismāʿīlīs and Khurramiyya on, 11–12, 94; in doctrine of Jaʿfar al-Ṣādiq, 78; in Khārijite doctrine, 55; in doctrine of followers of Masʿūd b. Qays, 66 and n. 54; in doctrine of Pārsiyān, 11; and the Thaʿāliba, 60; in Zaydī doctrine, 86–7
Imāmiyya, 30, 77–86, 92
īmān (faith): in doctrine of Karrāmiyya, 40; in doctrine of Mukram b. ʿAbd Allāh al-ʿIjlī, 62; in Murjiʾite doctrine, 15; in doctrine of Yazīdiyya, 75
India, 27, 49, 51, 52, 68, 70, 101
inheritance, 72, 88
initiation: in Ismāʿīlī doctrine, 100
interpretation: metaphorical, 28, 41; symbolical, 100
iqrār (verbal affirmation): in doctrine of Jahm b. Ṣafwān, 17; in doctrine of Karrāmiyya, 40; in Murjiʾite doctrine, 17
irjāʾ, 19, 21; condemned by Ḥanbalism, 23
ʿĪsā b. ʿAbd Allāh b. Saʿd, 79, 81
ʿĪsawiyya, 75–6
Isfahan, 27, 33, 34, 35, 36, 48, 49, 75, 97
Isfandiyār b. Adharbād, 97
Isfizār, 69, 70
Isḥāq, son of Saʿd b. Mālik b. ʿĀmir al-Ashʿarī, 79
Isḥāq b. Maḥmashādh, 44
Isḥāqiyya (= Murshidiyya), 49
Ishmael, 96
Islam: loyalist, 22; traditionalism in, 21–2, 27, 29
ʿiṣma (perfect immunity from error and sin), 78
Ismāʿīl al-Qaṣrī, 52
Ismāʿīl b. Aḥmad, the Sāmānid, 26, 30
Ismāʿīl b. ʿAlī al-Sammān, 30, 91
Ismāʿīl b. Jaʿfar, 80, 93
Ismāʿīliyya, 11, 32, 92, 93–105; missionary activity of, 93–4
ʿIṣmat Khātūn, 35
Iṣṭakhr, 76
istiṭāʿa (capacity to act), 65
istiwāʾ (God's rising above His throne), 41
ittiḥād (mystical union with God), 52

Jabal al-Rass, 87
Jābir b. Zayd al-Azdī, 73
jabr (determinism), 29, 63
Jadd, 94
al-jadīd (the 'new' teaching of al-Shāfiʿī), 26
Jaʿfar, brother of ʿAlī b. Abī Ṭālib, 7
Jaʿfar al-Ṣādiq, 46, 77–8, 80, 84 n. 24, 93
Jaʿfar b. Abī Yaḥyā, 91

Ja'far b. Muḥammad al-Nayrūsī al-Ṭabarī, 87
Ja'far b. Muḥammad b.Samā'a, 80
jahl (ignorance [of God]), 62
Jahm b. Ṣafwān, 17, 29
Jahmiyya, 29
Jalāl al-Dīn Ḥasan, 103
jamā'a. *See* 'charismatic community'
Jāmāsp, 96
Jamshīd, 11
Jarīr b. 'Abd Allāh, 79
al-Jarrāḥ b. 'Abd Allāh, governor of Khurasan, 15–16
Jāshan, 69
jazā'ir (provinces), 99
Jerusalem, 39, 45
Jesus, 75, 94, 97, 98, 99
Jews, 3, 75
jihād, 25, 48
Jīruft, 58
jizya (tribute), 16, 17; exemption from, 15; and the Soghdians, 14, 18
Judaism, 1, 75, 97, 98
Jūr. *See* Fīrūzābād
Justānids, 87, 88
justice, divine, 67
Juwayn, 69
al-Juwaynī. *See* Abu l-Ma'ālī al-Juwaynī
Jūzjān, 17, 45, 60, 87

Kābul, 70
al-Kalābādhī, 47
kalām, 28, 29, 30–31, 38, 42–3; Imāmī, 82–3
Kalār, 87
Kan, 91
Kantā, *see* Kanthā
Kantaeans (= Kanthaeans), 3
Kantayē (Christian term for Mandaeans), 3, 4
Kanthā, temple of the Kanthaeans, 4
Kanthaeans, 3–4, 5, 6
al-Karābīsī. *See* al-Ḥusayn al-Karābīsī
Karkūya, 70
Karrāmiyya, 33, 39–46, 91; legal and theological doctrine of, 40–43; and monasticism; 45–6; persecution of, 45
karūbiyya (Cherubs), 95
Karūkh, 69, 70
Kāshgar, 31
Kavādh, Sassanian monarch, 1
Kaynāniyya (= Kanthaeans), 4
Kaynawiyya (= Kanthaeans), 4
Kaysāniyya, 77: origins in the Khurramiyya, 7
Kāzarūn, 48–9
Kāzarūniyya. *See* Murshidiyya
Khalaf, 65–6
Khalafiyya, 65–6, 67
Khālid al-Qasrī, 58, 62
khalīfa (lieutenant): of the Mahdī, 80; of the absent Imam, 96, 99–100
khāliqiyya (God's eternal power to create), 42 and n. 12
khāliqūqiyya. See *khāliqiyya*
khānaqāh (convent): history of, 45–6, 45 n. 28, 49; and the Murshidiyya, 48
Khāqan of Türgesh, 17
Khārijism, 54–76, 86. See also *barā'a*
Khaṭīb 'Abd al-Karīm b. 'Alī b. Sa'd, 49
Khayāl, 94
al-Khayrānī, 82
Khāzimiyya, 58 n. 19, 63–5, 63 n. 40, 65, 66, 67
Khidāsh, nickname of Muḥammad b. 'Alī, 8
Khidāshiyya, 8
Khīwa, 52
Khotan, 31
Khujandī family, 35
Khurasan, 13, 15, 16, 21, 22, 52, 53, 60, 63, 73–4, 87, 96
Khurramdīniyya. *See* Khurramiyya
Khurramiyya, 1–2, 7, 8, 77, 94; hedonism of, 5, 12 n. 28; and

Rustamids, 73, 74
Rūyān, 87, 89, 92
Rūzbihān al-Fārisī, 52

Sabians, 75, 98, 99–100
Sabzavār. *See* Bayhaq
Saʿd Tamīm, 56
Saʿd b. Mālik b. ʿĀmir al-Ashʿarī, 79
Sadighi, H., 9
Sadīwar, 68 n. 67
Ṣadr al-Dīn ʿAbd al-Laṭīf, son of Ṣadr al-Dīn al-Khujandī, 36
Ṣadr al-Dīn Abū Bakr Muḥammad b. ʿAbd al-Latīf al-Khujandī, 36
al-Saffāḥ, 71
Ṣaffārids, 68
Ṣafī al-Dīn al-Wāʾiẓ al-Balkhī, 18
Safīdrūd, 88, 89
Ṣāhak, 76
al-Ṣāḥib b. ʿAbbād, 30, 90
Sahl b. ʿAlī al-Rāzī, 81
Sahm b. Ghālib al-Hujaymī, 56
Saʿīd al-Naḥwī, 15
Saʿīd b. Ismāʿīl al-Ḥayrī, 44
Ṣāʿidī family, of Nishapur, 32–3
Sājids, 71
salaf (pious ancestors), 43
Salamiyya, 93
Ṣalīdiyya, 67 n. 64
Saljuqs, 32–6, 45
Salm b. Sālim al-Balkhī, 21
Salmān al-Fārisī, 10
al-Ṣalt b. Abi l-Ṣalt, 67 n. 64
Ṣaltiyya, 67 n. 64
Sāmānids, 30, 88, 89
Samaritans, 3
Samarqand, 16, 26, 31, 38, 44, 49, 50, 51, 84, 85
ṣāmit: in Ismāʿīlī doctrine, 94
Ṣandaliyya *madrasa,* 37
Sanjar, sultan, 37
Sarakhs, 22, 60
Sāvah, 84
Sāwa, 36
al-sawād al-aʿẓam ('the great mass'), 20
al-Sawād al-aʿẓam, 20, 30, 39, 43
ṣawmaʿa (monastery), 46 and n. 31
Ṣaymara, 29
Sayyārīs, 47–8
Schaeder, H. H., 3
Sebüktegīn, the Ghaznawid, 44
Sem, 94
Seth, 94
settlers, Arab, in eastern Iran, 19, 21, 22
sexuality: in doctrine of Budayl, 10; of Khidāsh, 8; of Ṣiyāmiyya, 4
Shabīb al-Shaybānī, 70
al-Shāfiʿī, 26, 27
Shāfiʿism, 26–9, 31, 33–7, 91; and Sufism, 46–7, 47 n. 33, 48, 51, 53. *See also* factionalism
al-Shahrastāni, Tāj al-Dīn, 1–2, 4, 5, 6, 40, 41, 43, 59 n. 26, 60 n. 32, 65 and n. 49, 66 n. 55, 67 n. 62, 68, 71, 104
Shahrazūr, 56
sharīʿa (religious law), 99, 100, 102, 103; abrogation of, 10, 75, 94, 103; exemption from, 68; relaxation of, 104
Sharon, M., 8 n. 21
Shāsh (Tashkent), 26
Shaybān b. ʿAbd al-ʿAzīz al-Yashkurī, 62
Shayban of Bakr, tribe of, 70
Shaybān b. Salama, 60–61
Shaybāniyya, 60–1
Shaykh-i Murshid. *See* Abū Isḥāq al-Kāzarūni
Shīʿa, 30; extreme, *see* caliphate; *rāfiḍa,* 33
Shiʿism: and the ʿAbbāsids, 23–4; and conversion, 31; radical, 7, 80; sectarian development of, 77–81; and Sufism, 46, 52–3. *See also* Imāmiyya, Ismāʿīliyya, Zaydiyya
Shiraz, 27, 48, 101
shirk (polytheism), 67, 71–2, 76; see also *dār shirk*